What people are saying about

Capitalism on Campus

Making unique links between higher education and commercial sex, this book pushes the boundaries of both economic thinking and the politicisation of our universities. A much needed critique of what has become of our universities, which lays bare the bleak scenario for students. Engaging commentary is backed up by detailed reflections on the empirical knowledge we have on student sex work. This is essential reading for those concerned with economics, politics and student life as we enter new territory in both education and the sex industry.
Professor Teela Sanders, University of Leicester

Robert's text provides an accessible expose of the impact that market relations have upon British Universities and their students and makes a significant contribution to the body of work concerned with students' involvement in the commercial sex industry. Highly recommended.
Dr Billie Lister, University of Hull

Capitalism on Campus

Sex Work, Academic Freedom and the Market

Capitalism on Campus

Sex Work, Academic Freedom and the Market

Ron Roberts

Winchester, UK
Washington, USA

First published by Zero Books, 2018
Zero Books is an imprint of John Hunt Publishing Ltd., No. 3 East St., Alresford,
Hampshire SO24 9EE, UK
office1@jhpbooks.net
www.johnhuntpublishing.com
www.zero-books.net

For distributor details and how to order please visit the 'Ordering' section on our website.

Text copyright: Ron Roberts 2017

ISBN: 978 1 78535 800 5
978 1 78535 801 2 (ebook)
Library of Congress Control Number: 2017957744

A CIP catalogue record for this book is available from the British Library.

Design: Stuart Davies

Printed and bound by CPI Group (UK) Ltd, Croydon, CR0 4YY, UK

We operate a distinctive and ethical publishing philosophy in
all areas of our business, from our global network of authors to
production and worldwide distribution.

Contents

For Merry, Subira and Wandia with love.

Writing is about keeping a record and producing a kind of register of life
Les Back

There is hope outside this manifestation of the world that we know
Franz Kafka

Preface

In the opening scenes of Mike Nichols' acclaimed film *The Graduate*, a young Dustin Hoffman in the eponymous title role utters the immortal line, "I'm worried about my future." Several decades on, the graduates and would-be graduates of the world have been given no grounds for allaying their anxieties as they step uneasily into the future. The structures, forms and functions of higher education since Benjamin Braddock left his college books behind, to be bedazzled and confused by the sexual initiation proffered by Ann Bancroft's Mrs Robinson, have changed beyond recognition, as has the relationship between higher education and the sexual adventures and misadventures of students.

Differences between the US and the UK systems have narrowed in recent years. Mass participation was a feature of US higher education long before this became the favoured option in the UK, with private enterprise the foundation on which it was built. In the US, 63 per cent of higher education institutions are in the private sector;[1] not so the UK, where until the latter days of the twentieth century a system of free, fully-funded public higher education, replete with grants for students, functioned well for those who successfully negotiated the rituals of A-levels to enter the hallowed halls of academia. One of the aims of this book is to explore the nature of the transformed higher education landscape – where universities have disappeared and reappeared as de facto corporations. Another is to examine how this transformation is not only linked to the seemingly unrelated world of sex work but how the two industries pursue common aims through common means. In both, financial "success" is to be garnered by the manufacture and production of simulated pleasurable experiences. Both students and institutions now sell their wares on the open market and position themselves as

1

commodities for sale. That is, operating from the same premise, both sell "pleasurable", "fake" experiences – one sexual and relational, the other educational. That sexual satisfaction and student satisfaction have become market bedfellows should come as no surprise when one considers how students' presence in the world of sex work is driven by the same forces which have led to the privatisation and corporatisation of higher education. The same forces (austerity, financial fragility, commoditisation, the consumptive culture) and ergo the same or similar effects (maximisation of income, the body of knowledge and the body of pleasure as merchandise) have been brought about through similar means (marketing, emotional labour and the sale of "satisfaction"). This entangled, though taboo, relationship between higher education and the sex industry mediated through the financial colonisation of subjectivity means that it is pertinent to speak of the sexual economy of higher education.[2] After spending a good deal of the past 20 years undertaking research into students' mental health and their participation in sex work, all within the new financialised world of higher education, the pages which follow are a concerted attempt to address the nature of the relationship and of the taboo surrounding it. It is a document for our times even as the hours and minutes devour our collective memories and the present disappears quicker than ever.

This imbroglio of higher education and the sex industry can further be linked to the psychologisation of everyday life. This prime role for psychology in the exploitation of our individual and collective moods and wants was the subject of an earlier book (Roberts, 2015). There I sketched out the principal areas in which this forced marriage of convenience between the behavioural sciences and high finance has been enacted, alongside a potted history of scientific psychology's dash for cash. But the full story of this is far from told and if we wish to truly appreciate how the fabric of our private lives is now the principal means for fuelling the capitalist juggernaut, an examination of the calamitous state of tertiary education in corners of the Western world (notably the UK and the US) is necessary. It provides a fitting illustration of how large sections of the economy are currently predicated on exploiting and extracting wealth from the population in exchange for corporate construed happiness – the "inner light of universal benevolence" as Huxley (1994, p.70) envisioned it in *Brave New World*. Emotional labour, the manipulation of moods and desires is now central to the global economy. It has gone well beyond the "meat market" which Laurie Penny (2011) deftly examined.

Beyond documenting and analysing higher education's journey into market hands and the sexual sell-off of students, which is co-dependent on it, this book raises critical questions about the relationships past, present and future between education, learning, intellectual freedom and the cultivation of resistance to capitalism. The post-war fairy tale of education as a path to liberation is over. This does not mean that its emancipatory potential has been exhausted, transported to some pedagogical twilight zone, but with capitalism surviving in what some mainstream economists see as its final phase, it is imperative that we reimagine it and prepare for a life beyond it.[3] Teaching and research have always played a role in reproducing, in each generation, the core tenets of capitalist realism but that is by no means the whole story. At their best both create alternative and unforeseen visions of how the world is and can be. This power has been the main reason why business and government have sought to tame it and turn science and art into the distorted alienated practices for which they are too often mistaken.

Education has always had an ambiguous relationship with liberation movements, described by Back (2016, p.81) as providing "the tools of freedom and opportunity...organised in ways that make them also sources of 'indignity'". So, education is simultaneously desired and decried – deemed a necessary rite of passage to a better and more informed life but also perceived as a luxury for the privileged, as something distrusted and at odds with everyday working-class life. Witness, for example, the disparaging language of "ivory towers", of the term "academic" used to mean being of no practical importance and "nerd" as a term of abuse. One can trace this tension to the Cartesian split between intellectual and physical labour embodied in the division between the owners of capital and the power of the human labourers on which it is dependent. The bodies of students, employed for the sale of sexual services with the money accrued used to pay for their education, are a contemporary expression of the same problem. The body sacrificed to feed the life of the mind. It is time that this fractured relationship between the physical and mental sides of life was ended but in the ongoing war with capital, that victory is not yet in sight. The present book is a dispatch from the front lines of one of the ongoing battles – one that is drawing in increasing numbers of people, their families and friends. I hope readers find it enlightening and useful.

Acknowledgements

Thanks to my great friend Merry who as always has helped me with reading, discussing and editing what follows. She has also helped with the impossible task of adapting to the disintegrating status quo. Thanks to Chris Hewer for support and discussion over many years and to Teela Sanders, Linda Cusick and Billie Lister who all, at various times, offered me generous support and advice in the face of corporate hostility. A thought too to all my friends who still labour in the bleak houses of the contemporary university.

The upside-down world rewards in reverse: it scorns honesty, punishes work, prizes lack of scruples, and feeds cannibalism
Eduardo Galeano (1998, p.5)

Chapter One

The Death of the University

The idea of the University as a place of civic education and critical enquiry has been put to a premature death by a raft of neo-capitalist political rationalities that promote inter alia *divisive competition, false economies and philistine instrumentality*
Bailey, 2015

Money can't buy a thought, or a connection between ideas or things
Back, 2016, p.23

In the magic realist world woven by Gabriel Garcia Marquez, we learn that the convergence of many chance events makes absurdity possible. This is also true in the real world, though absurdity there can also have ostensibly rational origins. The process of reducing the function of UK institutions of higher learning into one geared to the exchange of commodities, a specialist branch in the art of possessing things, can arguably be traced to the late 1970s (Furedi, 2011). This was the time when Margaret Thatcher and her entourage began setting about the British economy with the sledgehammer principles espoused by the Chicago School of economists – first piloted in Chile, in brutal fashion, via the CIA-sponsored removal of the democratically elected government of Salvador Allende. The imposition of market reforms recognised as quintessentially neo-liberal arrived shortly afterwards and disaster capitalism was born (Klein, 2007). In the higher education sector, Thatcher's aim was to introduce an explicit market-oriented discipline into the workings of universities and the people within them. With the lady from Grantham having forsworn the existence of society – in her view "only individual men and women and families" existed

– the abstract was sacrificed for the concrete and the hapless student was now "expected to serve as the personification of market pressures" (Furedi, 2011, p.3). Thus was the student as consumer born and a raft of measures designed ultimately to ease money from students' (and their parents') pockets, trailed in its wake. Table 1 below shows a timeline of the key political changes in the funding of UK higher education.

Table 1. Political Changes in UK Higher Education Funding[4]

1981 Full tuition fees introduced for foreign students.

1989 Student grants are frozen, with yearly reductions of 10%. Student loans introduced.

1996 Dearing Report Commissioned.

1997 Dearing Report recommends students pay 25% of tuition.

1998 Introduction of **£1,000** tuition fees. Mandatory student grants are abolished and replaced by means-tested student loans. Described by Liberal Democrat leader Charles Kennedy as "one of the most pernicious political acts that has taken place".

2001 Labour re-elected with manifesto pledge to not introduce top-up fees.

2003 Fees are raised to a maximum of **£3,000**. Iain Duncan Smith pledges abolition of tuition fees under the Conservatives and calls them "a tax on learning".

2005 Almost all fees set at **£3,000** per annum.

2008 National Union of Students drops its opposition to tuition fees.

2009 Fees increase to **£3,290** per annum. Student loans are frozen.

2010 Browne Review recommends abolition of direct funding for arts, humanities and social sciences and reduction for other subjects. Abolition of tuition fees cap.

2011 Fees increase to **£3,375**.

2012 Fees increase to maximum of **£9,000** per annum plus **£5,500** maintenance loan.

Residents of Wales and Scotland entitled to free tuition within their own countries.

2015 Removal of maintenance grants for poorest students.

2017 Universities permitted to raise fees to **£9,250** per annum contingent on "high teaching quality".

Final confirmation of the triumphant incursion of market values into the UK higher education wonderland arrived just before the millennium in the form of the Dearing Report (National Committee of Inquiry into Higher Education, 1997). This set out the UK government's "vision of a learning society", one which envisaged students making "a greater investment in their own futures". Investment, of course, can take many forms – and as the language of the market grows more pervasive – a "deeply shared and transcendent faith", according to Seabrook (1990, p.11), "capital investment" has come to denote a world beyond the purely financial, embracing social, biological, cultural and human resources. The phrase "human resources" carries multiple meanings – from the human "capital" available to an organisation to the individual capabilities possessed by an individual. Normally these two different connotations would point to quite different interests. Sadly, in the environment in which academic staff and students now find themselves captive, the two have merged into one with the result that both academics and students see the need to sell themselves to those who wave the magic money wand. Their respective positions in the hierarchy of power mean that the choices available to them for doing this are not the same. The game, however, is that we are all for sale – perhaps a closing down sale for higher education as it once was or was ever thought to be. The underlying logic of the UK reforms is to replace government block grants to universities

9

and instead loan the money to students as an investment in their own "human capital". In this warped view education is construed as conferring no benefit beyond the individual person who has paid for it. The self-evident absurdity of this proposition should be obvious to anybody who has ever consulted a doctor, nurse, dentist or lawyer to name but a few of the professions which depend on university training.

Changes in the political funding of higher education have been accompanied by the introduction of a raft of "disciplinary" marketing instruments beginning with the Research Assessment Exercise (RAE) in 1986, followed by the Teaching Quality Assessment (TQA) in 1992, and the National Student Survey (NSS) in 2005. By the time the latter had entered the fray the conversion of universities from seats of learning into profit-making enterprises was complete. The RAE mutated into the Research Excellence Framework (REF) in 2014 while the TQA was exhumed and recast as the Teaching Excellence Framework (TEF) in 2017, reframing university education as something akin to an Olympic sport in which successful institutions could be "awarded" Gold, Silver or Bronze ratings.

The above changes have facilitated the corrosive branding of British universities – witness endless, witless mission statements, websites overrun with "badges, stickers and logos" (Scott, 2017) and endless verbiage couched in a higher education version of Newspeak, promising to "enhance" the "student experience" to undreamt of heights. Like Orwell's original in *1984*, the present educational dialect functions to suppress independent thought and, as in Aldous Huxley's dystopian novel, places the pleasure principle at the apex of human achievement. I will return to this issue in subsequent chapters, specifically to draw parallels with that which students who work in the sex and adult entertainment industries are endeavouring to produce in their clients. The community bound together by the new higher education language game is an administrative cohort –

"bureaucratic Rottweilers now snapping at all our heels" (Evans, 2004, p.3) able to see nothing beyond the power of money; an elite conforming to Kafka's portrayal as being "fleetingly glimpsed", "unassailable" and seemingly "governed by mysterious laws".[5] As surely as the language game binds management, accountants and advertisers together, however, it alienates and perplexes academic staff.

One of the many absurd aspects of the commodification of student life, though a recurrent and predictable feature of the impact of capitalism on all human affairs, is how activities and processes are turned into things. Verbs usually better suited for talking about these come to be replaced by nouns, a reflection of the tendency for capitalist social relations to objectify and reify all forms of human encounter, an issue which the psychoanalyst Erich Fromm (1976) critiqued many years ago. The emphasis on "experience" as a product to be bought and consumed, for example, is found in the packaging of adventure holidays and activities in the sport and leisure industry. It is the final frontier of capitalist excess and a sign that the barrier to the internal conscious world of the human "consumer" has finally been penetrated by the dollar.

So it is with the NSS that a student's experience of a whole range of issues connected with higher education will ultimately be reduced to a single score on an ordinal five-point scale: the different subjects they study; the various staff who deliver lectures to them, or mark their work, and who interact with them with varying degrees of efficiency and regularity; the nature of their relationships with these different staff; the efficiency of administrative support; the availability and standard of technological resources; library facilities; availability of up to date and historical literature whether books or journals; the nature of relationships with other students; the availability of leisure facilities, clubs and societies, how their life in general is going and so on. Furthermore, this score is somehow supposed to equate to the quality, depth and breadth of education one is receiving. The reality is that it functions as the universities' weapon of choice in the search for market share (Lenton, 2015). That such a score is divorced from any assessment of what input a student is making into their own learning or the wider economic, social and familial context in which they live only compounds the absurdity.

The NSS process can be likened to judging the outcome of a physical fitness programme on a group of people while ignoring the question of whether anybody ever shows up at the gym. Reading for a degree has given way to "getting" one – an entity that one buys which is delivered after a wait of 3 years. Brown (2006) argues, as have many critics, that NSS scores lack legitimacy, that they mistake access to information with its quality and carry the presumption that students are not just making meaningful judgements about the educational process they are engaged in but that all the significant effects of their university education can be assimilated and appraised before their degree course has even finished. Were it remotely possible to validly condense all the aspects of higher education life into a single score of satisfaction, this score would tell us nothing of any significance. It should not be necessary, but unfortunately, with universities having reached escape velocity from reality, it is necessary to say it: how satisfied one feels with whatever has transpired in almost 3 years of study, cannot and should not be taken as some proxy for intellectual rigour, critical thinking, educational worth, the effort the student has devoted to their study, how well they were taught – nor the relevance and applicability of what has been learnt to life. As if to confirm this, the pursuit of satisfaction ratings has resulted in many institutions investing heavily in landscaped campuses, sports and social facilities, marketing and public relations staff (McGettigan, 2013; Cocozza, 2017) – a case of never mind the quality, pay for the myth. With this the betrayal of the idea of the university is complete.

The TEF excepted, all the above measures have been directed towards ranking university departments and academic staff on a crude unidimensional scale – an "absurd and obscene system" in the opinion of sociologist Les Back (2016, p.63). Central to the audit of research and the hypothetical measure of its quality has been the process of assigning "impact factors" to journals, a dubious practice described as "psychometric nonsense" by Hartley (2012, pp.330-331) and "deeply flawed" by Schekman (2013).[6] Hartley considered the process intrinsic to the "McDonaldization" of higher education while Schekman, a Nobel prize winner, went further and suggested the pursuit of impact factors has "become an end....as damaging to science as the bonus culture is to banking". When assigning impact factors, an oddity seldom remarked upon is that greater weight is granted to publications specific to the North American continent. This arises because of the greater size of the North American market. One consequence of this – certainly in the social sciences and humanities – is that pragmatic considerations dictate that scholars are under pressure to express their views in ways consonant with the tastes of journal editors there. As with the NSS, the obvious conclusion (one to have escaped the attention of successive governments and those members of the academic fraternity who've sold their soul to corporate governance and agreed to participate as judges in this process) is that as instruments purporting to measure "quality" they all lack the one quintessential property which all metrics are supposed to possess – which is demonstrable validity. In one of the few robust analyses of NSS scores Lenton (2015) concluded from the results that the scores should not be used as a method of ranking not least because the students' satisfaction scores appear to be in large part markers of their "readiness and confidence to face the labour market" (pp.126–127).

A curious side note in the history of these metrics concerns the notorious publisher and former owner of *The Daily Mirror* newspaper, Robert Maxwell. Maxwell was a key player in the global expansion of academic publishing, turning it into "a spectacular money-making machine that bankrolled his rise in British society" (Buranyi, 2017). He managed this through his ownership of Pergamon Press prior to its later acquisition by Elsevier, currently the largest scientific publisher in the world. Maxwell's unique contribution was to recognise the enormous potential for profit in academia, driving up prices and convincing scientists that a given field required a new journal to showcase their work. With the number of journals proliferating, Maxwell's next trick was to insist on grand titles for them – "The international journal of..." was a favourite prefix. This public relations trick helped to cement the idea of a publishing hierarchy – so that whereas at one time all journals were held to be essentially equal, after Maxwell's intervention it was a case that some were "more equal than others". The notion of an "international" standard of research became a badge of honour and in due course was incorporated into the metric used in the first RAE. What this meant in practice, however, was far from clear, nobody being quite sure what counted as "international excellence" or what was understood by quality of research (see Alldred and Miller, 2007 for a summary of the confusion). By 2008 the phrase "international excellence", in common with most advertising slogans, had lost some of its earlier vitality and found itself relegated to a lower place in the hierarchy of esteem – to be supplanted by a new gold standard of "world leading", this being no better defined than the benchmark it replaced. One can only suppose that in years to come the descriptions will, like the Starship Enterprise, head out into the galaxy to set a new benchmark of cosmic excellence and take the insatiable hunger for profit to where no one has gone before.[7]

Understandably, researchers have felt compelled, for the sake of their careers, to conform to the "market discipline" which these metrics impose. This has had a far-reaching influence on the nature of academic discourse itself. The University and College Union (UCU), which represents academic staff throughout the UK, considers this to have had:

> a disastrous impact on the UK higher education system leading to the closure of departments with strong research profiles and healthy student recruitment. It has been responsible for job losses, discriminatory practices, widespread demoralisation of staff, the narrowing of research opportunities through the over-concentration of funding and the undermining of the relationship between teaching and research. (UCU, 2008)

Under this system, viable research is that which attracts the attentions of academic entrepreneurs and corporate sponsors. As Naomi Klein (2010) noted in *No Logo,* resistance to this market dominance of the campus has been minimal. In my own discipline of psychology "brain research, forensic psychology and behaviour genetics" are pre-selected for favourable ratings while investigations in the social arena are out of favour. Thus, the "psychology of political protest" and research directed towards the misbehaviour of political elites would be scored badly.

The changes in the UK environment are echoed in other parts of Europe. Faced with a restructuring of global capital markets and the birth of neo-liberalism in the late 1970s, many European governments decided that the university is obliged to become a partner in the wholesale transformation of capital markets. The ostensible aims were to increase the proportion of graduates in the population so that a more skilled literate workforce would be on hand to meet the challenges flowing from the changing (global and technological) nature of economic production. This, so the argument went, would serve to enhance national and international competitiveness. This philosophy is enshrined in the Lisbon declaration of the European University Association (2007). While this document calls for greater autonomy and diversity on the part of universities, it has if anything produced the exact opposite – having become a key driver of the restructuring of university life throughout the European continent towards a business-friendly bureaucratic agenda.

The document explicitly called for a bigger role for private finance, one that went hand in hand with a greater input from employers into the strategic aims of universities. These were accompanied by exhortations to promote "mission statements", "enterprise" and "knowledge exchange" paving the way for a radical transformation in the view of education. The once prevailing view that study and learning was of intrinsic value has been replaced by one in which its value is instrumentalised and costed. Within this framework the corporate mission reconfigures the role of students. In this pedagogical prison, thinking, learning, creating and performing serve only to produce graduate jobs or corporate profit. "Student outcomes" is the new mantra, both within and outside the university. Thinking for oneself and understanding the nature of the society we live in are reduced to externalities in this model. In the classrooms and lecture theatres, precise "learning outcomes" must be specified in advance and listed in the curricula like items on a fast-food menu, to be later spat out undigested at exam times and then forgotten. No unexpected surprises are permitted. The micro-management and surveillance of teaching and learning does not stop there. After graduation, monitoring systems continue to track employment rates – information to be assimilated and incorporated into next year's brochure.

If one wishes to gain an understanding of the state of the modern European university subsequent to these developments, Tucker (2012, p.12) provides a damning perspective. In his view universities are now hostages to market imperatives and stand at the mercy of reforming neo-liberal governments. In this environment, the management of higher education has become obsessed by quantity not quality, with the university on a seemingly unstoppable conveyor belt to intellectual stagnation.

> The corporations...tell the public universities what kinds of specialists they need, the universities...produce them, and the graduates will have an excellent chance to work for the companies. The state will collect and spend taxes, and the corporations will save on the costs of training new employees. However, the interests of the big corporations are not identical to those of students and workers. Corporations prefer to receive welfare from the public purse to save on their training expenses; they prefer highly specialized workers who can start work immediately and cannot change jobs easily. Workers who are overspecialized cannot find alternative jobs easily and therefore occupy a weak negotiation position. If they lose their job when the company collapses or contracts, they have a limited set of skills to offer other employers.

It is not hard to conclude from this that academic self-governance along with its once treasured freedom has been abolished. In place of our old universities there are now factories of learning – the new dark satanic mills run by managers who follow a model "that resembles the late Soviet model of industry during the Brezhnev era" (ibid, p.102). Tucker describes this managerial class as "failed academics and clerical and secretarial staff" (p.108) – a description from my own experience that is particularly apt (of which more later).

The collapse of the ivory towers as places of free thinking and intellectual liberty could easily lead one to surmise that the university has reached the same state of obsolescence as the family in David Cooper's (1971) eyes, God in Nietzsche's and the Parrot in John Cleese's – that is that it is in effect dead. The university, God and the parrot are alike in another manner in that there are people with vested interests in believing in their existence. Inevitably these interests are financial – the university sector in the UK was estimated to be worth over £73,000,000,000 per annum in 2011–2012 and to generate over three quarters of a million full-time jobs, around 3 per cent of all UK employment (Universities UK, 2013). How the UK's expected departure from the European Union in 2019 will affect these figures is currently unknown though the prevailing view beyond the party champions of EU exodus suggests there will be significant adverse effects, many of which are at the time of writing already being felt. Unable to acknowledge the death of the university publicly we are condemned to live in a state of lucrative[8] denial as unwitting students and their parents support the lavish lifestyles of the teams of bureaucrats who maintain the government/corporate simulacrum that animates the corpse of the actual deceased university. It is neither in a state of rest nor pining for the fjords; it passed beyond life-support a while ago. All that remains is a symbolic fiction. The burden of paying for higher education has in the corporate makeover been transferred from the state to individual students – at least in theory, though in practice a high proportion of students in the UK never attain the critical levels of income after graduation to begin paying back their loans.

Some disciplines have borne the brunt of the corporate assault more than others. Research by the Universities and College Union (see Bailey and Freedman, 2011) indicates that social science subjects have been particularly hard hit, with all public funding for arts, humanities and social science subjects scrapped. It is important to stress that it is not just that the funding model for higher education has been altered. The notion that day-to-day academic life somehow continues unabated and undiminished through these changes is a fiction.

Tucker (2012, p.118) continues:

The centrally managed university is a parody of a university, a Potemkin village that has the facade of a university. Instead of teaching, it has cheating; instead of Socratic dialogues, it has bullet points; instead of a community of scholars united by a search for truth, it has atomized individuals suspicious of each other and informers for the manager; instead of intellectual and spiritual life in truth, academic life is devoted to the implementation of absurd, senseless, immoral, and harmful policies that percolate down through an anonymous, unaccountable bureaucratic hierarchy.

This bureaucracy functions, as Kafka instructs us all bureaucracies do, as an instrument of terror, exposing in its wake "manifestations of ignorance and incompetence in the university's administration" (Parr, 2014, p.7). In this vein Tucker suggested that some academics have seriously entertained the notion that the plethora of reforms across the European continent have in fact been designed to make public higher education so intolerable for the academy's inhabitants that when universities are eventually privatised, everybody will breathe a sigh of relief rather than take to the streets.

One of the customary demands of any terror apparatus is for those subject to it to sacrifice their grip on reality. Publicly endorsed principles, for example of academic freedom and tolerance for diversity of opinion, may be abandoned at a stroke in the actual day-to-day running of the institution with concomitant denial that anything is amiss. On one occasion one of the managerial apparatchiks of the institution in which I was working remarked to me (delivered with insincere bonhomie) that "just because I've written something (in an email) doesn't mean you should assume that I believe it".[9]

How exactly can one, as both employee and human being, respond to this? To engage in open conflict is to risk being shipwrecked in a sea of gobbledegook, caught in an endless current of trying to make sense out of something which, from the recipient's point of view, essentially lacks it. If we take seriously the proposition that UK higher education now functions as a hyper-real simulation of a previously historically existing structure of "real" higher education, then we are led to the realisation that to work within it is to be entangled in a fantasy system no less complex than that found in the dysfunctional families described in the writings of the Scottish psychiatrist R.D. Laing, a veritable phantom zone where intellect, culture and politics are all denied (see Faulkner, 2011). Another possibility, theoretically at least, is that the university is a nostalgic simulation of an institution which has never actually existed but which is believed by many to have been real in the past. The relatively recent rise of managerialism ought to rule out this idea as there are still enough people alive who can recall the flawed reality of the past. In our political desires to resurrect and reclaim the university in a future free from the clutches of the monster, we must be vigilant against the lures of a pre-neoliberal nostalgia. The academy has long been a home for privilege – of class, gender and race. They "were not admirable institutions" (Evans, 2004, p.3). To save the university from the present we must take great care in how we look back.

It hardly needs pointing out that customary belief in the existence of the university as a real thing is founded upon several apparently incontestable factors. Thus we are likely to believe that we are working in a university if there is a believable hierarchy of academic prowess on show; that is, that there are students, lecturers and professors, that the lecturers are suitably qualified, teach and do meaningful research in areas of their choosing; that is, pursue academic freedom and challenge existing wisdom; that the students study, engage in debate, take exams which are fairly assessed and so on; that there is in addition a suitable physical geographical infrastructure such as libraries, computers and lecture halls and that these are appropriately used. Each institution will also have its acquired history and roll call of illustrious alumni to make everything appear that much more credible. The internalisation of the relationships between these actors, institutional artefacts and institutional history is what forms the basis of the belief that the university is in some sense "real". But what if all is not what it seems and the image fails (either wholly or in part) to map on to reality. Roberts and Hewer (2015, pp.175–176) elaborate:

What if professors do not hold high academic qualifications or are not leaders in their field? What if principles of meritocracy are abandoned in favour of other political or social criteria? Having relatively low achievers at the helm may produce an organisational culture that makes it difficult for academics to do research, given the bureaucracy created by those who are not research active. High fliers in the research game, instead of being rewarded, pose a threat to their underachieving superiors and therefore research is constrained and subtly discouraged, so that a conflict ensues between what is said through every organisational channel of corporate communication and the daily experience of academic staff. Some universities may perceive the principle of academic freedom as a threat to deeply held political beliefs or policies. Consequently, there may be a widening disparity between the collective fantasy, publicly presented, of the university as a dispassionate seeker of truth and its existence as a corporate entity seeking to satisfy its consumers in order to survive.

The preponderance of many low achievers in senior positions gives rise to what has been humorously described as "Kakonomics"[10] – the strange preference for low quality outcomes. This is envisaged as a theoretical game (a variant on the prisoner's dilemma if you like) in which high achievers receive few if any rewards for work beyond their own intrinsic motivation while a class of low achievers risk few sanctions while being open to high rewards. Two Italian academics (Gambetta and Origgi, 2013) outline the game play, one which leads to a scenario in which the field is run by "self-interested individual defectors and 'cartels' of mutually satisfied mediocrities". What they are defecting from is a commonly believed standard of high performance. They cite the example of a secretly recorded university appointments committee in Bari celebrating how they had "screwed" one candidate – overlooking them for another whose citation record was inferior by a factor of six. Such aspiration to mediocrity is not confined to the "bel paese".[11]

The Canadian scholar and cultural critic Henry Giroux (2014, p.79) lamented: "All too frequently positions of academic authority have been awarded to opportunistic careerists who remain completely untroubled by the burdens of complicated thought and the fight for ethical and political responsibility."

My own experience would suggest this type of behaviour is common in academia – hard-wired in fact into the DNA of universities up and down the length and breadth of the UK. It is not difficult to find professors, heads of school, deans and pro vice-chancellors who lack the basic rudiments of a successful publication record. One notorious example from the UK illustrates both Kakonomics and the shortcomings of the NSS in one fell swoop. In 2008, two academics at Kingston University in London were recorded encouraging students to effectively falsify their ratings on the NSS (BBC News Online, 2008, The Telegraph, 2008). In the recording, which can be found on the Wikileaks website (https://wikileaks.org/wiki/Kingston_University_National_Student_Survey_fraud_recording) one of the two staff, Dr Barlow-Brown, could be heard telling the students: "If Kingston comes down the bottom then the bottom line is nobody is going to want to employ you because they are going to think your degree is shit, all right?"

According to the BBC, she went on to say:

In effect, you're competing against lots of students at other institutions who also want their university to look good... Although this is going to sound incredibly biased, you rate these things on a five-point scale, if you think something was a four – a "good" – my encouragement would be give it a five, because that's what everyone else is doing.

Her colleague, Dr Vallee-Tourangeau, said the survey was no place for students to vent "garbage" about how they disliked their courses. Although then Vice-Chancellor Sir Peter Scott described it as an "isolated incident" it is clear from the comments posted below the article, from students at several other UK universities, that putting pressure on students to give favourable ratings is not uncommon and is well understood. Furedi (2011, p.5), for example, has written of institutions adopting practices that "border on bribery to get undergraduates to give the right answers to student satisfaction surveys". Although the episode at Kingston led to the university being barred from the NSS the following year, it didn't seem to do the careers of the two any harm. Dr Valllee-Tourangeau was subsequently promoted to Professor and Dr Barlow-Brown to Associate Professor – despite in Dr Barlow-Brown's case having a publication record (two papers in the last 20 years) which can only be described as threadbare. Contrary to what must be the expectations of many readers it is unarguable that many of those occupying elevated academic positions at UK universities have very poor publication records. The truth is that these positions and academic titles are frequently given as rewards to those whose area of expertise consists of shuffling bits of paper around, attending a few committee meetings and demonstrating a willingness never to question any decision that comes down from on high, no matter how dubious. Not so much a case of "publish or perish" as perhaps don't publish *and* relish the consequences. To save numerous individuals, many of whom could easily be named, the embarrassment of exposure, I'll leave it to the interested reader to scour the web pages of any number of university departments and discover the unpalatable truth for themselves.

The existence of cartels of mediocrity raises interesting questions about organisational behaviour. What threshold, in terms of the number of people, is required for one to become viable in an institution? And once there, how does it develop, sustain and consolidate its influence? One may suppose that the essential tactics for any medium to long-term stability of such a grouping must involve influence over the comings and goings of staff – likely exercised by control over the hiring process – shortlisting and interviewing – and the exercise of force; that is, bullying to direct people towards the exit door. Then there is the question of the topological organisation of the cartel – whether and how far it operates over distinct layers of the organisational hierarchy. What heights in the organisation must it reach to secure its position and power? These are all suitable research questions for how the modern university operates, to not only entrench mediocrity but maintain a neo-liberal consensus. Henry Giroux links this squarely with the political and moral environment engendered by neo-liberalism: "All too frequently positions of academic authority have been awarded to opportunistic careerists who remain completely untroubled by the burdens of complicated thought and the fight for ethical and political responsibility (Giroux, 2014, p.79)."

One could easily lengthen the list of accusations against the market-contaminated university. For example, what if the actions and functions of the supposed academic hierarchy have more in common with the running of a supermarket chain than an institute of learning? And what if the central planners behind the current set up don't want academics to do research, and in fact detest "unfettered scholarly inquiry" and want vocational training rather than higher learning (Tucker, 2012, p.99)? What if the students don't study, what if the library has few books and journals? What if students don't write their own essays, and think they buy their degrees rather than earn them through their own efforts? In short, what if the whole enterprise is a gigantic lie?[12] Then there are the demands on the staff to internalise and exhibit unswerving allegiance to the institution. The dean of one institution in which I worked told me that I would not be considered for promotion because I had failed to display sufficient loyalty to the university. After further probing, the "deficiency" on my part was that 3 years earlier I had made a complaint against another member of staff – the dean's husband, in fact, who also just happened to be professor and head of school at the time. His rise through the ranks was obviously thoroughly merited despite the absence of a doctoral degree, and a list of publications which stopped short of the number three. Kakonomics seems omnipresent in UK university life and keeps on popping up when you least expect it, as do various scandals. While broaching the subject, one should always keep one's eyes peeled for news of one kind or another in the ivory towers – both here and across the Atlantic. Here, there have been many; accounts of vice-chancellors' expenses, severance packages (*Independent*, 1998) mismanagement (*Times Higher Education*, 2012), resignations (*Independent*, 2009a), NSS scores (BBC News Online, 2008), reporting of student numbers (Independent, 2009b), student enrolment (*The Telegraph*, 2012), promotion (*Times Higher Education*, 2011) and validation practices (BBC News Online, 2011a) are just a few to have graced the pages of the UK press. Many are kept hidden. The lengthy list of these scandals, redolent of a banana republic and suggestive of the unchecked entitlements of privilege, indicate something is seriously amiss.[13] Following the money and querying how power flows through the university are usually effective investigative strategies for discovering exactly what it is. Exhortations to loyalty can extend beyond institutional policy and practices to government policy, whether domestic or foreign. The largely uncritical domestic support offered by university vice-chancellors to tuition fee increases and marketisation[14] suggests not merely a lack of vision, and subservience but a propensity to keep one eye on the huge salary and another on possible later rewards from the honours system.[15] A disturbing illustration of pressure to conform to foreign policy agendas concerns the operation of Campus Watch, an organisation in the US, which has turned its ire on faculties who work in Middle East studies. Students have been invited to submit reports on professors whose views are considered dissonant, with dossiers on them compiled and distributed. It has been described as waging "a war on academic freedom" (McNeil, 2002) and has unmistakeable McCarthyite overtones. In the UK, the government's Counter-Terrorism and Security Act of 2015 imposes a statutory duty on higher education institutions to prevent individuals being drawn into terror (note that the potential causes of radicalisation are assumed to be wholly unrelated to foreign policy). The fear associated with the directive concerns the manner in which academics are expected to comply with it, for example by vetting visiting speakers and reporting on student behaviour. Such actions are likely to not only be counter-productive but will also likely threaten open debate and freedom of speech and alienate students (See UCU, 2015).

It is undeniable that since the "end of history" proclaimed by Francis Fukuyama, history has changed and with it the higher education landscape in a form beyond recognition. Warped by the transforming power of corporate desire, a lust for learning has given way to a lust for money, power, market share and social control. Given this, ideas of what a university is are changing and with this gaps are opening-up between the present reality and the decades (if not centuries) old social fantasy of university as a democratic home to society's dispassionate truth seekers. How far this fracture between fantasy and reality can proceed before the casualties become undeniable is hard to discern.

The less socially desirable, secret life of the institution is kept under wraps by several means. Internal disciplinary measures and threats carry a certain weight, though one must also consider the desire not to know – to deny that a standard bearer of British culture for centuries is rotten to the core (See Cohen, 2001 for a wider discussion of denial). Then there is the compliance of the Press. A piece I submitted on the widespread corruption and nepotism present in higher education for the "Academics Anonymous" blogspot in the UK's *Guardian* newspaper, was, after initial interest, rejected once it reached the editor's desk. No explanation was given. Reading what does get accepted produces an impression, difficult to shake, that a more suitable running head for this column would be "Middle-Class Academics Anonymous" who don't wish to dig too deep. Alas it's too long and not as catchy.

One cannot be surprised, however, at *The Guardian*'s reluctance to air the corrupt consequences of the neo-liberal order when it has been a vocal champion of it. Every year its nonsensical league tables and prizes for "teaching excellence" are force fed to its readers and drooled over by university administrators and publicists for all their worth – which is not very much.[16] In this endeavour to compare the workings of UK academia with football's Premier League, *The Guardian* competes with *The Times* which employs a completely different algorithm when it comes to distinguishing the winners from the losers.

This, however, isn't the whole story. The pursuit of mediocrity and league-table performance do occasionally clash, albeit in a surreal manner. I know of at least one institution where a departmental head was promoted to associate professor following a precipitous drop down the league tables – to the bottom of them in fact, following an 18 percentage point fall in NSS scores in a single year – equivalent to over two standard deviations (Lenton, 2015). A Kafkaesque example perhaps of damning with faint praise.

To continue to consider today's modern university as a standard bearer of enlightenment values, while possessing full knowledge of its neo-liberal workings requires something akin to hypnotism. This might not be far from the truth as its nearest scientific equivalent, Neuro-Linguistic Programming (NLP), has, in some establishments, become a tool in the armoury of academic managers to badger staff into obedient behaviour. Still the situation hasn't yet reached that in some secondary schools where teachers are being offered Electro-Convulsive Therapy to combat stress and depression (Jarvis, 2017) – an approach described by the trust promoting it as "dynamic and forward thinking".

Threats, fear and NLP work to produce compliance internally – but what about externally? Here, the said supportive behaviour of the wider press has been noted. This works hand in hand with public relations departments and press offices – the universities' very own "adjustment bureau" to maintain the set of necessary illusions.[17] Accordingly, the self-anointed institutional heirs to the enlightenment are subject to regular make-overs. To keep up appearances, universities as they now construct themselves in their own brand image are in the "business" of selling themselves to prospective students, their parents and big business for their own survival. This they do in a not dissimilar fashion to some of the students who populate the landscapes of higher education. Such market activity one can argue constitutes a greater peril to esteemed Western pedagogical values and our remembered way of life than anything Buffy the Vampire Slayer dispatched in her regular battles with the blood-sucking demons on campus who were, it must be noted, like university administrators, conspicuous in their abundance.

This turn to the power of the image to promote universities has had far-reaching consequences, one of which is that the illustrious alumni associated with a given institution are often celebrity figures from the wider pop culture. But this can be a two-edged sword, uncontrollable to a degree, with the cool and the cruel often recalled in the same breath. Thus, do we find that Dave Gilmour of Pink Floyd fame formerly attended what is now the University of Westminster, as did the knife-wielding murderer we know as Jihadi John. *Careful with that Axe, Eugene,* one of the Floyd's most famous compositions, echoes synchronously and uncomfortably across the temporal air waves as a result.

The salience and importance of image to the campus managers can lead to head-on clashes between the marketised university and its supposed mission to extend knowledge and critical thinking to the wider world. One area where this clash has been acute revolves around another facet of capitalist excess in the ivory towers – the participation of students in sex work. This will be the focus of the next chapter.

Embarrassment is risky and unstable; it has to be handled with tact but without reverence
Svetlana Boym, 2017, p.93

Chapter Two

Economics, Politics, Student Sex Work

*Back when I was a student I listened to a lot of Hot Chip and fucked
a lot of guys for money. I basically have a degree in fucking. I have
a proper degree too, on our much-loved English language and
its lofty literary heritage. I got a first. Higher education taught
me how to use my tongue in every sense, from clever syntax to
cleverly working it around wherever I was paid to do so. These two
qualifications are not unconnected*
Lees, 2014

*In my day, people went to university in order to avoid this kind of
life, but now they lead this kind of life in order to go to university*
Female Massage Parlour Owner in Leeds, BBC World Service
interview with the author, 2001

In the not so distant past, students were commonly perceived to
see out their study years in semi-permanent states of debauchery
and revelry, with few cares or responsibilities. This romanticised
perception is nowadays rarely articulated, at odds with the high
stress, high debt, high-pressure environment that many find
themselves in. When I began researching students' lives in the late
1990s, market reforms were still in their infancy. The abolition of
mandatory grants and the introduction of the first tuition fees by
New Labour (set at £1,000) did not take place until 1998. There
were few indications of the level of economic disorder that was
about to come crashing into students' lives. Few – but they were
there and one didn't need a crystal ball to see them. Just as I
was putting the finishing touches to the design of a survey on
student health and well-being I came across an anecdotal report
in *The Times Higher Education Supplement (THES)* (Barret, 1997) of

students becoming involved in prostitution.[18]

On reading the report in the *THES*, my colleagues and I added a single item to the survey. Unsure of what would be deemed permissible by an ethics committee at that time and hardly anticipating what we would turn up, we decided to ask whether respondents knew of any students (male or female) who had engaged in drug dealing, prostitution or crime to help support themselves financially. When we came to analyse the results (data had been gathered from almost 500 students from three different universities in the south east) we were struck by several key findings. First, we found that a substantial proportion, almost three quarters, were experiencing financial problems such as difficulty in paying bills – the figure was even higher for students who were parents. Second, we noted that just over 3 per cent reported knowing someone involved in prostitution and third, that people were over three times more likely to report this if they themselves were in debt – a statistically significant association. This was the first hard data to suggest that students were engaged in sex work and that this participation was linked to financial problems (Roberts et al., 1999; Roberts et al., 2000). The data also suggested that students' mental health was adversely affected by the amount of debt they had accrued and the long hours they worked to support themselves.[19]

If we are to understand the student presence in the global economy of sexual-service provision then we must begin with an account of the forces which led to its emergence in the first place. Although this tale will be largely confined to how events have unfolded in the United Kingdom, it mustn't be forgotten that student participation in the sex industry has been documented across several continents – North America, Australasia, southeast Asia and throughout Europe (Roberts, Jones and Sanders, 2013; see also Lantz, 2004; Sedgman, 2004; Weitzer, 2000; UCA News, 1999). The common factor behind this geographic spread is the globalisation of higher education markets, itself one aspect of contemporary capitalism's drive to "liberalise" all economic activity. Prime targets for this have been the range of welfare and education services provided and regulated by the state. Marginson (2006) notes how universities in the US, UK and Australia played leading roles in the development of a commercial mass market in higher education, constructed initially around elite institutions in these countries, which paradoxically stand to be the most sheltered from the raw effects of marketisation.

Running parallel to the assault on free public higher education is a timeline of escalating student debt (see Table 2 below) which shows a rise from just under £5,000 in 1997 to an estimated £50,000 by 2017 – the highest in the English-speaking world. These soaring levels of personal debt are accompanied by increases in the time expected to pay them off. It is widely accepted that most students will never pay off the debts they've accumulated, impacting on their disposable income and their ability to access affordable housing among other things. The picture of a corporatised higher education system, correlated with rising student debt, is completed by the increased participation of students in the sex industry over the same period (see Table 3). Seeing a correlation between the geography and scale of student sexual commerce and the (re)modelling of students as customers and consumers of educational services is hard to avoid (see Sanders and Hardy, 2013).

Table 2. Mean UK Student Debt Since 1997

1997 **£4,800** (Swanson, 1997).

1999 **£5,248** (Barclays News release, 2000).

2004 **£12,180** (NWB, 2004) – a 50% increase over previous year.

2007 Those starting their course estimated to graduate with **£21,000** of debt (BBC, 2007).

2011 **£21,198** (D'Arcy, 2011).

2012 Institute of Fiscal Studies (Crawford and Jin, 2012) estimate that tuition fee increases will increase the average student debt by over £19,000.

2013   A student on a 3-year course with tuition fees of £9,000 a year and receiving a maintenance loan of £3,575 would leave with a debt of **£43,515** (Prestridge, 2013). By 2015 it is estimated that the average graduate debt will have risen to 169% of the average starting salary (Wexo, 2013).

2014   A student on a 3-year course with tuition fees of £9,000 would leave **£44,035** in debt (BBC News Online, 2014).

2016   Graduates who've paid fees up to £9,000 a year are estimated to have left university with an average debt of **£44,000**. Student loan debt rose to £86,200,000,000 as the first cohort to face fees of £9,000 graduated. It is estimated that two thirds of UK students will never pay off the debt. Total US student debt is $1,400,000,000,000, although the average debt per student is greater in the UK (Tetlow, 2016). Degree debt in England is now the highest in the English-speaking world.

2017   Student loan debt has reached over £100,000,000,000 (Monaghan and Weale, 2017). Institute of Fiscal Studies (IFS, 2017; Adams, 2017) indicates average debt on graduation is **£50,000**. Students from the poorest 40% of families entering university in England for the first time in September 2017 will leave with an estimated average debt of **£57,000**. Students from the richest 30% of households would run up an estimated **£43,000** of debt. Three quarters of students will never fully repay their loans. Scrapping of bursaries for student nurses and midwives.

Table. 3 Student Participation in Sex Work: A Timeline of Research

Barret (1997) First anecdotal evidence of students engaging in prostitution.

Times Higher Education (2001) Evidence gathered by Leeds University Student Union from sex worker support services estimates 60% of sex workers in Leeds are students.

Roberts et al. (2000) 3.1% reported knowing other students involved in prostitution to pay off fees.

Roberts, Bergstrom and David La Rooy (2007) 10.5% report knowing other students involved in sex work to pay for their education (lap dancing 6.3%, stripping 4.2%, escorting 6.3%).

Roberts, Sanders, Myers and Smith (2010) 25.7% indicated they knew of students involved in some type of sex work (non-internet pornography 5.4%, internet pornography 7.3%, escorting 9.8%, stripping 12.1%, lap dancing 18.1%) to pay for their education. 16.5% of students indicated that they would be likely/very likely to participate in sex work.

The English Collective of Prostitutes (2011) note a doubling in the number of calls received from students in the past year. The group said there had been a steady increase over the past 10 years.

Sanders and Hardy (2012) report 87% of their sample of lap dancers had completed further education, 23.2% had completed undergraduate education, 5% had completed postgraduate education, and that 29% of dancers were engaged in some form of education.

Sagar and Jones (2012) Student Sex Work Project Begins – a 3-year project funded by the BIG Lottery. Action research project aims to promote learning and understanding about student sex worker needs and motivations, and provide an innovative sexual health service to a marginalised population.

Roberts, Jones and Sanders (2013) 30% indicated they knew of students involved in some type of sex work. Around 6% report working in some branch of the sex industry.

Sagar et al. (2016) Student sex work project survey of several thousand students indicates over 5% have worked within the sex industry.

Student Money Survey (2017) In a cash crisis 5% of students turn to "selling their body".

The Research

This first study, conducted in 1998–1999, set the ball rolling for what was to follow. In the post-1992 university where some of the work had been conducted, it soon became evident that conducting further research in this area would be difficult. Furthermore, and not surprisingly, when word filtered out, the UK government did not welcome the findings.[20] Questioned in the House of Lords during the early part of 1999 about the implications of the findings, higher education minister Tessa Blackstone responded:

> I do not believe that the study adequately attributes stress and poor health to financial problems; it does not really make the links. However, that does not mean that the Government should not be very careful to look at the impact of the new arrangements. My department has asked for research based on a very large sample – 2,000 full-time and 1,000 part-time students – to be undertaken this summer. We shall be reporting on that study next spring...We shall certainly want to look at any health problems experienced by students. (*Hansard*: Session 1998–1999, 4 March, columns 1791–1793)

Despite Blackstone's promise, the government neither undertook nor reported on any study commissioned into links between students' financial circumstances and their health. Nor did the British Press evidence any interest in this broken promise. This avoidance set the tone for institutional responses from government, universities and the National Union of Students for years. I will discuss these in some detail in the following chapter.

On the academic front, initial publication of the data was followed by an invitation to a conference on College Health in

San Diego. There, I was surprised to learn that what was news in the UK was considered unsurprising in the US even if it was not publicly acknowledged. Several of those attending the conference independently told me that they knew people who had put themselves through medical school, at least in part, by escorting. The existence of a pattern of widespread debt from self-funded university education, associated with the take up of sex work to meet the economic demands of study, is apparent on both sides of the Atlantic and in fact throughout the world. Indeed, it can hardly be considered surprising – the US model of higher education stands as the global standard and so when we imported that model we imported the consequences that go with it.

What was becoming clear was that compared to the usual array of poorly paid jobs, working in the sex and adult entertainment industry could be advantageous for students in terms of time and money for their studies (Lantz, 2004; Moffat and Peters, 2004; Sedgman, 2004). With this early research, and a rising tide of anecdotal evidence, the need for further study was pressing. Getting it done, however, was proving to be difficult (Roberts, Bergstrom and La Rooy, 2007a). About 5 years later we managed to conduct a small-scale study investigating the pathways towards sex work. Again, we employed indirect measures of involvement to circumvent some of the obstacles and practical difficulties (Roberts, Bergstrom and La Rooy, 2007b).

This second investigation provided further evidence of an association between sex work (defined in this study as prostitution, escorting, lap dancing or stripping) and students' economic circumstances (the amount of debt, difficulty paying bills and hours worked). It was noted that over 10 per cent of respondents knew of other students engaged in sex work – up from the 3.1 per cent observed in the first study. In discussing the significance of the findings, we raised several points which remain relevant today; that the role of financial hardship in contributing to mental health problems in students is one which the authorities appear to take little real interest in and that the relevant stakeholders in UK higher education (government, Universities UK and the National Union of Students (NUS)) have shown little inclination to recognise or address the problems that are on their doorstep.[21] Concern with this latter point prompted Linda Cusick, Susan Patton and I to ascertain what exactly were the policy positions of UK higher education institutions with respect to student or staff involvement in commercial sex. We wrote to all 326 higher (HEIs) and further education institutions as listed by The Higher Education Funding Council for England and the Scottish Funding Council. Of the 236 who replied (72 per cent) none had any policy prohibiting staff or student involvement in commercial sex, although many pointed to unwritten assumptions which could be used to penalise legal but stigmatised sexual behaviour – justified in the eyes of the institution because of implied threats to a university's "image or position". Cusick et al. (2009, p.191) commented:

It is also clear from the dominance of discussion about disciplinary procedures and behaviour bringing institutions into disrepute that staff/student participation in commercial sex is widely perceived as some kind of institutional threat... As with all responses in this category, institutional letters referring to policies on harassment or bullying did not give any information on why these policies might be relevant. This is interesting because, whereas the tone of these letters again suggested an intolerant view or punitive response, the harassment and bullying policies support individual privacy. Certainly, unwanted enquiries about one's personal or sex life are described as harassment and the person making remarks or asking such questions would fit the descriptions of harasser as set out in the submitted policy documents. Hence, any institutional enquiry into the circumstances of staff/student involvement in commercial sex would itself be prohibited under these harassment and bullying policies.

The disregard shown by universities for the rights to privacy of staff and students involved in commercial sexual activities, which are perfectly legal, in favour of a disciplinary moral stance which owes more to the sensitivities of tabloid journalism, ought to be considered highly disturbing. From the perspective of an enlightened liberal democracy it is this abandonment of concern and respect for individuals whose work and study forms the lifeblood of the university that arguably constitutes actions with the potential to bring the institution into disrepute. We live however in the upside-down world described by Eduardo Galeano (1998) where those with power routinely turn reality on its head. The collection of institutional responses makes one thing abundantly clear – that the neo-liberal obsession with "student satisfaction" takes second place to the institutional satisfaction with neo-liberalism. Corporate image as ever trumps welfare.

Media interest in student sex work, meanwhile, was growing (for example, Brinkworth, 2007; Dolman, 2008) as academic interest appeared confined to a small set of people – a few interested and committed students, myself and several colleagues from the sex work research community who provided valuable support and encouragement. Faced with continuing difficulties in getting work done which would provide us with more detailed information about student sex work, we decided to explore students' attitudes and perceptions towards it in the context of a growing acceptance and mainstreaming of sexual labour outside the ivory towers. This has been most evident with lap dancing's ubiquitous presence on the high street and despite financial hardship and vulnerability being the central reasons for entering sex work, it has not been restricted to women (and men) from working-class backgrounds. Influenced by Bernstein's (2007) perspective on the "new respectability" of the sex industries among the middle-classes – a respectability which opens up possibilities for new types of worker and customer to enter sexual commerce, the next study (Roberts, Sanders, Myers and Smith, 2010) delved into the attitudinal environment in which students make sense of working in the sex industry.[22]

In this investigation – with over 300 students – we employed both qualitative and quantitative means to tease out students' views. On the qualitative side, we posed a series of open-ended questions which dealt with respondents' views of student participation in the sex industry, why they thought students participated, how participation was thought to affect students and what the NUS and universities could potentially do to support those working in it.

Many of the students considered participation a personal choice, deemed reasonable so long as it was safe and lacked coercion. Others, however, denounced the sex industry as "disgusting" and "immoral", said that those working in it have "personal issues" (for example, being lazy and greedy) but that situational factors such as lack of money, available jobs or support were instrumental in pushing people into it. Interestingly, safety concerns were brought up by only a handful of respondents, while one differentiated between activities in the sex industry; with prostitution equated with "lower standards", while "dancing" was considered "ok" so long as the person doing it was "confident"...a suggestion perhaps of the route by which erotic labour has been normalised. In all, over half the students found it easy to understand how others ended up working in the sex industry. When asked to give reasons why they thought this occurred, four main themes emerged; money, sexuality, despair and personal context. Money was overwhelmingly given as the main reason (by 93 per cent of respondents) with debt, bills and student fees frequently cited. Several referred to working in the sex industry as a "convenient" means to make easy and quick money – a recurring motif in much of the research that has been

40

conducted both before and after this study. A few referred to students' personal circumstances as possible motivating factors – for example, "low self-esteem", "family problems", "peer pressure", "lack of guidance" and "unfortunate circumstances".

When it came to what the NUS and universities could do, the majority view was that they could do more to support students participating in sex work. Five clear types of support were suggested: prevention, health promotion (including counselling and support groups), financial support, career support and research. What is striking about this list is that as far as universities and the NUS in England are concerned, they have done little or nothing with respect to any of the items. Only around one in five universities for example have specific sexual health clinics for students while outside the sector, NHS sexual health services have faced draconian cuts. The students' calls for further research have moreover generally been met with an icy reception by both institutional players (see Chapter 3).

When we looked at the quantitative data, we found one in four respondents (25.7 per cent) knew students engaged in sex work – a marked increase from the 3.1 per cent observed in 1999/2000 and the 10 per cent in 2007. Pole dancing (18 per cent), stripping (12 per cent) and escorting/prostitution (10 per cent) were the most frequently reported types of sex work which they knew other students were doing. We also found, consistent with Bernstein's argument about the mainstreaming of sexual consumption among the middle-classes, that students from middle-class backgrounds were the most likely to report knowing other students who were involved.

In a further sign of the normalisation of attitudes to sex work almost one in six (16.5 per cent) admitted considering some type of sex work, with debt and understanding students' participation in it two of the factors likely to predict this stance. We concluded the study by considering the possibility that selling one's labour in the sex markets may become a feature of the mainstream rather than alternative informal economy and that understanding students' career trajectories into and out of these markets was now vital (see Sanders, 2007). In our final words, we noted:

> There is clearly a relationship developing between sex work, student financial survival strategies and debt. Appropriate responses are required from organizations that represent either students (for example, the NUS) or those that have a duty of care and benefit from their presence (the universities)...For action to take place, both the NUS and universities must be prepared to acknowledge the issue to a much greater extent than they have to date by adopting a more open and accepting attitude both toward sex work and toward students who feel this is a necessary course of action for them. (Roberts et al., 2010, p.154)

Although this work was widely reported and I conducted several media and radio interviews (for example, BBC News Online, 2010), no positive responses were forthcoming from any of the principal higher education stakeholders, as the BBC report cited illustrates: "A spokesperson for Bath University said: 'We have checked with both our Students' Union and with our Student Services department and neither feel that this issue is relevant to the University of Bath.'"

In turn, the UK government said only that "it provided 'generous' financial support". This is the kind of political avoidance that Theresa May, some years later, would turn into a cybernetic art. Meanwhile, evidence of the relationship between indebted students and sex work continued unabated. The English Collective of Prostitutes (2011) revealed that the calls it received from students had doubled in the previous year on top of a steady increase over the preceding 10 years. The group noted that it had received an unprecedented volume of calls since the government's announcement that tuition fee charges of up to £9,000 a year were in the pipeline for English universities (BBC, 2011b). In the US, two separate studies – by Girresch (2011) and Long, Mollen and Smith (2012) – obtained comparable figures for the proportion of students (28.4 per cent and 28.9 per cent respectively) who personally knew a sex worker, while Teela Sanders and Kate Hardy (2012) in the UK found over a quarter of the 197 lap dancers they surveyed were currently engaged in education and were using dancing as a strategy to support themselves. The main reasons given by the women were the excessive cost of higher education, the lack of available loans and the ability to combine stripping work with the educational demands they faced. Added to this, a Channel 4 News (2012) investigation pointed to the growth of "Sugar-Daddy" websites where "cash strapped young women", one third of whom are students, and these from some of the UK's elite universities (including Cambridge, Nottingham and Kent), were seeking mutually beneficial relationships with rich "sponsors". News of medical students working as escorts also began to appear (Anonymous, 2012; Dixon, 2012).

Thus, by 2012, several distinct studies had identified the push factors behind students' presence in the sex markets as the cost of higher education, financial adversity and the flexible work conditions available compared to standard labour market jobs. Given the crisis of replicating findings which is present in the social sciences this ought to have been considered impressive. However, academic scrutiny of the sexualisation of higher education was in danger of falling behind the media attention which closely followed it. The reasons for this will be discussed in the next chapter but what was needed now was some clear picture of the precise extent of the phenomenon. At this stage, all we had was suggestive but indirect evidence that the proportions of students engaged in sex work was increasing alongside student debt, and that it was widely understood and considered acceptable by students. However, we had no precise measure as to how many were involved and in what way. This was to come from three sources, two of them from the UK.

In a survey conducted with several hundred students – drawn from over 29 universities in the UK – Teela Sanders, Amy Jones and myself (Roberts, Jones and Sanders, 2013) sought to obtain data on the prevalence of student sex work and further our understanding of the pathways leading to it. Unnecessary delays (of several months) in obtaining ethical clearance meant we ended up with a much smaller sample than we had hoped for. In the results we obtained, financial problems were again widespread. Thirty per cent reported knowing someone involved in a branch of the sex industry to pay for their education. Six per cent indicated that they worked in either stripping, erotic dancing (lap/table/pole/topless dancing) or escorting/prostitution, the majority of whom said that they had confided in others about the nature of their work. Confirming the middle-class incursion into sex work, social class background appeared to be unrelated to participation in sex work as did the type of university attended (Traditional v Post 1992). However, sex workers reported being in more debt, and were more likely to have been in debt prior to the commencement of their studies. Some of the advantages of engagement in sex work were demonstrated; the weekly earnings of student sex workers were over four times greater than students doing other jobs. No clear picture emerged, however, of any psychological/mental health differences by the type of work students were doing.

In this study, we had also enquired into students' roles as purchasers/consumers in sex work/adult entertainment. Internet pornography was the chief activity (40 per cent) followed by visits to strip (24 per cent) and lap-dancing clubs (15 per cent) with only a small percentage (1.5 per cent) using escort agencies. Men unsurprisingly were more frequent consumers overall although the proportion of women consumers of some forms of sex work was marked – for example one in three had taken to internet pornography and about one in six had visited strip clubs or bars. As with sex workers, consumers evidenced no distinct psychological profile, though the levels of sexual "consumption" certainly points to a highly sexualised culture and a student culture within it subjected to the live now (desire and consume) pay (and suffer) later pleasure dynamic that saturates late capitalism. A potential danger in this scenario is that students living in the haze of this culture of immediate gratification, carrying substantial loans, with payback of their debt postponed beyond the immediate future, may be prey to the machinations of an industry seeking further expansion on the back of their future poverty.

One of the unanticipated findings was that those students who explicitly saw themselves as consumers in paying for their education were more likely to be among those who regarded participation in the sex industry as unacceptable. One possibility here is that the financial restructuring of higher education may be bringing in its wake a more conservative set of political attitudes, in that the more students adopt the identity of an educational consumer the more they absorb and adopt an attitude set, situated within a conservative moral universe. One of the implications of the noted prevalence of sex work was that students engaged in sex work to pay for their education were contributing an amount likely to exceed several million pounds annually to the higher education economy. We will consider this in more detail shortly. For now, these figures add weight to the view that the sex industries are "of major economic significance in the cultural capitalism of the twenty-first century" (McNair 2002, p.6), a conclusion reinforced by the robust evidence that these industries, particularly the strip-based industry, are strongly reliant on student labour (Sanders and Hardy, 2012). As Sanders and Hardy (2015) (see also Sanders, 2012) have demonstrated, students, along with migrants are a core group of young women who constitute a supply group of transient labour into the licensed strip industries of the UK. It is this group who often enter the strip industry for petty cash, attracted to the work more as a lifestyle choice where they can enjoy hedonistic pleasures of working in the night-time economy. In Sanders' view, these women, affected by the poor employment opportunities for graduates, may well end up staying much longer in sex work than they anticipated.

Work in Berlin (Betzer, Kohler and Schlemm, 2015) provided the first major systematic estimate of the prevalence of student sex work outside the UK. The German researchers found 7 per cent were currently involved or had been involved in the past, while one third had "imagined" doing so. As in the UK study of 2013, this was linked to financial adversity, sex workers receiving less financial support from their families and being more often in debt. The third pointer to the proportion of students involved in sex work would come from the *Student Sex Work Project* (SSWP) which began in Swansea in 2010 (Sagar and Jones, 2012; Sagar, Jones, Jones and Clarke, 2014). This has been the most ambitious and largest research project on student sex work to date; a 3-year partnership forged between Swansea University and Terrence Higgins Trust Cymru, the University of South Wales, the NHS Wales and the NUS (Wales).

Building on existing work the aim was to embed student sex work within a practical context concerned with developing interactive health services for student sex workers. The hope was that the research and practice would lead to policies and protocols which could be implanted into UK higher education to facilitate greater knowledge, improved sexual health and better welfare and support for students contemplating or engaging in sex work. One of the major contributions of this project was to interrogate the respective merits of contrasting paradigms of sex work – the worker as active agent or as exploited victim – when applied to the varied and complex lived experiences of student sex workers. The central goals of the study were to assess the extent of student involvement, how frequently or infrequently they participated, and to discern the nature of the motivations and experiences in it.

The main questionnaire phase of the study gathered data from over 6,000 students drawn from higher education institutions in England, Wales, Scotland and Northern Ireland. The survey yielded a figure for the proportion of students who had been involved in sex work which was comparable with previous estimates – in this case 4.8 per cent (Sagar et al., 2016). Just under half of these (2 per cent) were involved in the provision of direct intimate sexual contact – the bulk of these in escorting and selling sexual services independently in indoor premises. A much smaller number worked in brothels or massage parlours and a still smaller number had worked on the streets. Activities comprising indirect sex work (for example, internet/webcam sex, erotic dancing, stripping, phone sex) were the most frequent type of involvement. To some surprise the reported participation in direct sex work by males was greater than for females. This suggests two possibilities – neither mutually exclusive – that males were or are more likely to come forward to admit their participation or perhaps, more likely, that females involved in direct sex work were under-represented in the survey. Whichever is the case the overall estimates are broadly consistent with previous work and may even be an underestimate of the true extent of student sex work. Beyond this number who had been involved, a much wider number (22 per cent – again comparable to previous findings) had considered it.

With this figure and data on the numbers of full-time students in England, Wales and Northern Ireland (Universities UK, 2016), and the different fee levels in the three countries along with the numbers of higher education institutes in England (N=132), Wales (N=8) and Northern Ireland (N=4) which take full-time students, it is possible to calculate an average income per institution from students who are sex workers.[23] This comes out at between £5.16 million and £6.41 million.

Analysis suggested students' motivations could be reduced to two main factors – financial/practical considerations (for example, funding higher education, funding lifestyle, coverage of basic living expenses, avoiding debt, reducing money owed at the end of study, convenience afforded by working hours) and reasons intrinsic to the work itself (for example, an explicit desire to work in adult entertainment/sex work, anticipation of enjoying the work, sexual pleasure, curiosity). Positive elements of the work were given as good money, flexible hours, working conditions, freedom from employment regulations, sexual pleasure and good clients. Of the negative aspects, secrecy was the most frequently mentioned – others included unpredictable earnings, fear of violence, negative judgements from friends or family, lack of employment rights and a changing view of sex. Over three quarters reported feeling safe and only 8 per cent that they rarely or never felt safe. Most of those working did so for less than 5 hours a week, while just over half had been involved for under 6 months. There was considerable variation in the amounts of money earned – over half made less than £300/month while around one in seven earned over £1,000. As expected, those engaged in sex work spent significantly more hours on personal study – an average of over 4 hours more each week.

The major reasons given for leaving sex work could be grouped into several categories; stigma, boredom, the effect on relationships, prioritising education and moving area. The perceived difficulty of leaving was unrelated to monthly income or the frequency of support from family, parents or partner. It was, however, significantly related to support from friends. Over half (58 per cent) of those who sought frequent emotional support from friends reported finding it easy to leave compared to only 5 per cent who reported it as difficult. In addition, those engaged in prostitution reported more difficulty in leaving than other sex workers. Finally, and very importantly, several psychological and behavioural correlates of sex work were found, with sex workers reporting poorer mental health, greater alcohol consumption and drug use.[24]

In a second strand of research, the Swansea team (Sagar et al., 2015) returned to the question of how higher education institutions deal with students who take part in sex work. Little, it seemed, had changed. The research found that even though a good number of university staff had experienced student disclosures of their involvement, no provisions, policies or training had been put in place to address it. Furthermore, staff members' knowledge of the legalities of sex work and appropriate referral pathways was demonstrably inadequate. Some institutions and the staff within them cannot think beyond seeing student sex work as something that would bring the reputation of the university and/or the profession for which the student is training into disrepute – and thereby a subject ripe for disciplinary action. Thus, the hapless student is caught in the dynamic between two contradictory disciplinary forces arising from the dominant position of capitalism on campus. On the one hand, the entry of "market discipline" to all spheres of academic life and on the other, the scramble for market position and the perceived necessity to manipulate brand image to achieve it. Given the concern with student sex workers bringing certain professions into disrepute, the irony was noted that research has made links for many years between sex work and the caring professions – with testimonials from sex workers attesting to their role as sexual health educators and counsellors as well as pleasure providers. We will return to this issue of the body – and particularly the female body – as a politically-contested site and zone of political struggle in Chapter 4. A conservative reaction, however, was not the only response. In some institutions, staff acknowledged that an individualised supportive approach would be necessary, although they were mindful that they lacked the means and institutional backing to deliver it.

Making Sense of the Research

To make sense of the relationship between the marketised student and their participation in the sex industry, we need to understand the deep interplay between myriad social and cultural processes at large in the stagnating economies of late capitalism. At the time of writing the overall picture we have is of a sizeable minority of students participating in sex work; that economic considerations loom large in their motivations to do so; that the difficulties they experience are not only related to the work itself but also stem from the labour conditions and societal responses to it such as stigma and lack of support (for example, Sanders, 2004; Scoular, 2004; Krusi et al., 2012) and that the work offers distinct advantages (for example, money, time available for study, working conditions and enjoyment of the work). The final part of this picture is that tuition fees from students are keeping the higher education economy afloat, bringing to the fore the responsibility of educational institutions to respond pragmatically and to facilitate the provision of health, safety and welfare support to students engaged in or considering taking up sex work. This is hard to dispute.

What this review of the work documenting students' presence, purpose and plight in the emerging sex markets of the current era tells us is that the neo-liberal drive to dominate all aspects of human life – the basis for a veritable post-modern totalitarianism[25] – encounters no obstacles when it reaches the doors of academia. Students, refashioned as educational consumers, have thoroughly absorbed the monetary ethic and are wont to apply this to every aspect of their passage through tertiary education. Their world of study, social and sexual relations is now a minefield. In these overlapping worlds, they must battle, as no generation before them has had to, a ferocious complex of objectifying forces and do this amid a precarious labour market with youth unemployment rates across Europe at alarming levels. The objectification and commodification of human labour entails that all human capacities and possibilities can be envisaged as forms of capital. Sex work offers advantages of flexibility, temporariness and the possibility of a much greater income than typical part-time work. The "self-interested" student, captured in the vice of an expanding higher education market, contending with spiralling debt in a shrinking job market may, unsurprisingly, turn their hand to making money in whatever way they can (Roberts, 2010). It should be remembered that the numbers of students in the sex industry are to be seen alongside other "risky" financial activities such as gambling and medical experiments which they have also turned to (Sanders and Hardy, 2014). Rather than passing judgement based on an anachronistic Victorian morality this can be seen as "an act of resistance to the experience of relative poverty" (McLeod, 1982, p.26) and a marker of rational decision-making. The economic psychology of the contemporary student, thoroughly disciplined to market realities – and years of debt is a form of imposed discipline – has readily embraced capitalist mores, commodification and the buying and selling of sexual services. They are aware of the power of their own "sexual capital" and are prepared to exchange this in the same way as the higher education institutes which absorb their money and trade teaching, research and the body of knowledge for prestige, greater market share and their own survival. Both are engaged in the management of others' desires and the proliferation of "consumer" fantasies (see Haywood, Jenkins and Molesworth, 2011). For students, the prize is not just the acquisition of a degree, but also their own survival in a cut-throat economic world which demands they leap on the runaway train to endless consumption. The individual and social cost of this adaptation, both in the short and long term, are nowhere near to being known.

While cognisant of the socio-economic and cultural context within which student sex work exists, the human dimension must not be overlooked. Progressive arguments about sex work have claimed that it is just another form of work in which emotional labour is involved, and as such is in principle no different from other forms of work in the service industries which require it. Consider, for example, the empathic psychological work expected of air cabin crew, shop assistants, hairdressers, sales people, doctors, nurses and psychotherapists to name but a few. The importance of empathy, however, does seem to have been neglected by some state actors – those associated with administering welfare and benefits provision for example! The overtly moralising tone of the discourse which surrounds public consideration of the issues would, one might suppose, preclude the possibility that there could be any mutually beneficial human dimensions to the work. But research and the workers themselves tell a different story. Sanders (2008) observed that contrary to prevailing myths, client-sex worker relationships can be characterised by friendship, trust, emotional engagement, respect and intimacy and that "it's not always a bad thing" (p.206). The findings from the *SSWP* show that these possibilities exist there too, that students in the sex industry may sometimes enjoy their work as well as finding it challenging, unpleasant, necessary and profitable. That this is so difficult to entertain is one consequence of the habitual assumptions which most people employ when the subject of sex work is aired. Another is the stigma that perpetually resides in these assumptions and continues to surround sexual labour. There is nothing inevitable about this.

This must change if progress is to be made. A question for universities and for the NUS is why their members are increasingly turning to employment which entails the provision of sexual services to a paying public with the attendant risk of psychological, physical and future occupational harm to themselves. Another is how are they going to respond to this for the welfare of their students? The signs are not encouraging although there are university staff who recognise that they need greater awareness and training for dealing with their students – training that universities seem unwilling to provide despite their protestations of a concern for student satisfaction. There is a choice. On the one hand, they can opt to get behind the commodified fantasy of student satisfaction found in the NSS, or on the other they can follow the exhortations of Ewan McGregor in *Trainspotting* and "choose life" and by doing so put the real lives and welfare of students ahead of the demands of capital. Researchers in this field have sought to direct attention to the practical steps that higher education institutes and others can take, to not only recognise the issue as one of student welfare but as one replete with human needs that can be addressed.

With sex work routinely stigmatised and the people involved in it pathologised (Burnes, Long and Schept, 2012), the question as to how this pervading stigma affects the ability of academics to carry out the necessary research with students comes to the fore. It is also the type of issue which places academic freedom near the top of the list of the zombie corporate university's list of targets. In several places in this book I have alluded to difficulties faced when researching student sex work. The next chapter will examine the nature of these in some depth as well as the motives of those institutional players who are responsible for the obstruction.

All that once was directly lived has become mere representation
Guy Debord, 1992, p.5

Chapter Three

Researching Student Sex Work: Academic Freedom, Market Values

To meet the needs of the world around it, a university's research and teaching must be morally and intellectually independent of all political authority and intellectually independent of all political authority and economic power
1988 Bologna Declaration, cited in McGettigan, 2013, p 114

The ivory tower has now become the padded cell
Berger, 2016, p 156

The above statement, adopted by EU Ministers of Education in 1999, forms part of *The Magna Charta Universitatum* (Bologna Declaration). It was signed by 388 rectors and heads of universities from across the world on the 900th anniversary of the University of Bologna – the world's oldest university in continuous operation.[26] The document outlines principles of academic freedom, institutional autonomy and governance that have been consigned to the history book by UK vice-chancellors and managers. The indecent haste with which these guiding principles have been discarded and forgotten ought itself to be a subject for study in the academy. The present chapter forms a case study of the consequences which flow from the abandonment of academic freedom. First, it comprises a demonstration of how received wisdom (in this instance concerning intellectual freedom) can be seriously out of kilter with both the desires and the realities of a political economy centred on the well-being of a tiny global elite. Second, it signals a dangerous erosion of our taken for granted democratic values; a retreat from the core principles which a university is expected to advance and defend as part of a modernist project to nurture public space, free thinking and debate. Third, it suggests a perilous reworking of our own designated relationships with self, others and institutions.

The institutional policy framework towards staff and student involvement in sex work is, as we saw in the last chapter, punitive. For example, in Cusick et al.'s study of the regulatory landscape in UK higher education, disciplinary regulations or codes of conduct which might reference misconduct or bringing an institution into disrepute were referred to by 56 institutions. This strongly suggests a widespread institutional perspective which sees participation in sex work as inherently negative and potentially damaging (by association) to institutions of higher education. This goes some way towards explaining why there is such a paucity of academic research on an issue which is barely out of the news and which potentially involves and affects large numbers of people. There is a need, however, to go beyond this broad picture and ask how exactly this institutional hostility is translated into an unwillingness by academics on the ground to investigate the area. The following picture is one which I have pieced together – from my own experiences, from talks with several academics regarding the institutional "welcome" extended to their attempts to investigate student sex work and from a tiny external literature which has commented on the existent regulatory framework. It suggests two broad practices underpin the research neglect. The first of these concerns the active failure of powerful "stakeholders" to show any interest in the area.

Stakeholders, Sex Work and Politics

Three main stakeholders in question are the UK government, the NUS, as the body purporting to represent students, and lastly the universities. Successive governments' vested interests in avoiding scrutiny of the human consequences of their neo-liberal educational policies are not hard to fathom and have been discussed at length in the first two chapters. The NUS provides a further example of the destructive impact of neo-liberalism. As Kumar (2011, p.136) explains, the NUS has adopted "a corporate model, with the inclusion of external trustees – often business and university heads – in the most powerful union bodies... In recent years (it) has positioned itself as a national level lobbying group, with local unions as service providers, members as consumers, and democracy as expendable."

The NUS has come to the issue late, having for many years adopted an equivocal attitude towards student sex work. Individual women officers of the union have been helpful in disseminating Sanders and Campbell's (2012) work on stripping and in their advocacy for evidence-based approaches to support and guidance. *The Student Sex–Work Project* has also forged strong links with the NUS in Wales. The Women's Campaign and the LGBT+ campaign, working with the Sex Workers Open University and the English Collective of Prostitutes, also launched a small survey in 2016 to gather information on the lives and experiences of student sex workers (NUS, 2016). The intentions are good and contain some useful recommendations – for example for the NUS itself to offer greater support and advice to student sex workers, though unfortunately, the very small sample size and misrepresentation of some research has not been helpful.[27]

Overall, however, the official stance taken by the English NUS has been disappointing, repeatedly denying both the importance of the issue and that any meaningful research had been conducted in the area, not to mention pulling out of an earlier agreement to undertake a national study of student involvement in the sex industry, this a good 12 years prior to the *SSWP*. At the time (around 2003) I was informed that a decision had been taken by the president, above the heads of the welfare officers of the union with whom I had had several hours of constructive dialogue. I was informed that the president had issued express instructions that nobody was to talk to me. Two invitations by the NUS to speak at conferences on the topic were also rescinded without explanation. With so many past NUS presidents having moved on to lucrative positions in the main political parties – all of whom have supported the position that students must pay for their own training while rich banking elites are deserving of massive tax payer handouts – it is not hard to see where self-interest takes precedence over representing students' interests. The union's historical position on tuition fees is also one which sits comfortably with neo-liberal politics – it has since the mid-1990s accepted that students should pay towards their education. This has been described as offering "tokenistic resistance" (Kumar, 2011, p.135) to tuition fees and in 2011 it described the coalition government's higher education reforms as "relatively progressive" (BBC News Online, 2011c).

And then there are the universities, which have offered no constructive suggestions whatsoever. The response of universities to student sex work is best considered through three avenues. First is the disciplinary agenda surrounding student sex workers, second there are the attempts to obstruct, impede, hinder and discourage researchers from doing the work, and third the recourse to what is called reputation management if we are being polite and bullying on behalf of the "brand" if we are not. As we have already discussed the potential use of institutionalised disciplinary policies against student sex workers, the following discussion deals with the obstruction of research and the desire to protect corporate image which underlies it.

Obstructing Research

The primary tactic favoured by UK universities is to directly threaten academics that their careers will be adversely affected if they go ahead and do research – an operational philosophy of "publish and perish"! The fall-back option if this fails operates through the influence on local ethics committees. We'll consider these separately.

A. Threats To Career

Consider the following remarks made to me by a higher education manager:

> Where a member of staff's research does not contribute to the RAE, it is the [the management's] responsibility…to encourage the member of staff to undertake research which does contribute to the RAE, and therefore does generate income for the university and for the team. This in itself does not mean that a member of academic staff's research can be stopped, as long as it does not contravene normal ethical and institutional policies. It is entirely within that member of staff's power to continue with their chosen line of research. However, in that instance, they cannot expect additional research support intended to promote RAE performance and above the minimum granted to all staff. They must also take the consequences of their chosen line of research in terms of future employability…You must compromise your academic freedom. (Roberts, 2010, p.15)

This is not difficult to decode. Managers decide what work "contributes to the RAE" – now rebranded as the REF, a supposed system for measuring academic quality, in advance of it being done, prior to its later submission for peer review and possible publication. Such "decisions" cannot be judgements based on anything to do with the actual quality of work – intellectually or methodologically – as it may be assessed by other knowledgeable academics in the field. Such a judgement then, as a supposed measure of quality, has zero validity. This type of decision-making, however, is not unique in the neo-liberal university. What has just been described – a supposed estimation of the quality of a piece of work made before the work has even been done – isn't so different from how some institutions grade students' work – the average mark being decided in advance before work is read. The aim here is to artificially elevate students' scores, which it is hoped will increase their satisfaction and consequently the league-table position of the university (Cockburn, 2017). The economist Ray Bachan has provided convincing evidence that grade inflation in higher education cannot be explained by changes in the efficiency of teaching methods, nor by the factors which traditionally predict degree success (for example, prior A-level performance) or university characteristics (for example, old university v new university). Instead, he suggests "there may be a conscious effort by UK universities to lower...standards to attract fee-paying students" (Bachan, 2015, p.1593). It is difficult to see this as anything other than a form of corruption. As Marx said of capitalism – all that is solid melts into air – including it would seem standards of probity and academic excellence.

With regard to researching student sex work, the institutional benchmark for RAE/REF acceptability, referenced in the above letter, is not the quality of the work but the topic. The RAE/REF thus functions as a vehicle for instilling "academic discipline" – a means for ensuring that academics do not research the "wrong topics". In the resurrected moral Victoriana which comes with a return to the naked values of nineteenth-century capitalism, university students selling sexual services is judged to be the "wrong" topic. Exactly why we shall see shortly! The right topics presumably are those which raise money or support the corporate higher education agenda in some way – an agenda which values the private ownership of intellectual ideas, the banishment of critical thought and the acquisition of money ahead of traditional forms of academic output such as writing and lecturing. As Naomi Klein (2010) noted in *No Logo,* resistance to this market domination of the campus has been minimal – at least on the part of faculty. The student voice has been more vociferous in its opposition, notably to campus corporate partnerships. We have yet to see the corporate branded campus in the UK but many research positions, from fellowships to professorships, have already met this fate.

But it is not just the various research assessment inquisitions which have been used as a weapon to suppress free enquiry into students' place in the sex markets. Prospective PhD students in several institutions have been told that their academic careers will be stalled or buried entirely if they exercise their intellectual curiosity or passions in this direction. None of this gets reported, of course, and so a very effective realm of censorship reigns and the looking-glass university sees only its own reflection in the world it surveys as it grows ever more detached from reality.

Threats may also operate outside the immediate academic environment. In June 2013, *The Independent,* as part of a wider investigation into student sex work, ran a piece based on the work we had conducted on student attitudes (Roberts et al., 2013). This appeared on page three of the newspaper, trailed on the front page under the banner "SEX FOR TUITION FEES: ARE UNIVERSITIES REFUSING TO FACE UP TO THE FACTS?" (See Brown, 2013). The article mentioned some of the difficulties of getting work cleared through ethics committees and presented information that hundreds of millions of pounds a year could be going into the university coffers from the fees of students who work in the sex industry. The *"Indy"* subsequently let me know that Universities UK, who describe themselves as "the representative organisation for the UK's universities" had tried to get the story dropped. They argued "(t)he article will be very misleading to readers – including prospective students and parents…Following (this) piece, we intend now to raise this with the editor…"

Happily, Universities UK's attempt at "information management" was unsuccessful. The affair plainly illustrates the discomfort higher education elites feel about the interdependence of the economies of higher education and the sex industry becoming public. Supply side economics has rarely been so troublesome. Students supply their labour to the sex industry and their money to the universities. The comments from Universities UK are also revealing in another way. Their concern about higher education's image is principally directed to funders of overseas students and parents who support their offspring's education. Not only is this predicated on a repressive sexual morality but it also evidences a desire to maintain disinformation about the plight of students. So much then for the cherished notions of a free market! In the hallowed world of Adam Smith this is after all supposedly reliant on (rational) prospective buyers having complete access to all relevant information. Without it, the market is distorted. As the "customers" in this case – the students – are also those who are being exploited, the need to distort the market and maintain disinformation about their predicament is paramount. Hence the withholding of relevant information must encompass not only prospective levels of student debt and the job prospects associated with higher education but also the attendant social and welfare costs which include low paid work and entry to sex work. Under the neo-liberal economic model of higher education all potential costs to student well-being and welfare are to be treated as externalities and of no concern. As the sex economy grows and establishes itself in the consumptive mainstream, the subject positions of students in this *Paso Doble* economy resemble something akin to Shrodinger's famous cat – simultaneously the lauded "satisfied" customers of the NSS and the disowned "dissatisfied" purveyors of other people's sexual satisfaction in the hidden booming sex markets of England's green and not so pleasant land.

The day the story appeared in *The Independent* the message communicated to me was that "this has to stop". I was left in no doubt that this referred to the research and not the neo-liberal sanctioning of independent thought. In his foreword to *Brave New World*, Huxley (1994, xlviii) pondered the accomplishments of propagandists. Their dictum, "great is the truth, but still greater, from a practical point of view is silence about truth", is one with which Universities UK and the institutions whose interests they represent seem fully conversant.

B. The Ethics Committee

If overt threats fail to instil the necessary self-discipline then the coterie of academics who staff ethics committees can be relied upon to make life difficult. Ethics committees exist ostensibly to protect the welfare of research participants, a practice which can be traced to the development of the Nuremberg code in the immediate aftermath of World War Two. According to Adam Hedgecoe it has become a commonly accepted truth among sociologists that prior ethical review of research, a custom which began in the biomedical sciences, is unsuited to the oversight of social science. Academics from both the UK and the US have maintained that it is not only overly bureaucratic but can constrain the autonomy and academic freedom of researchers. To further his argument, that the proliferation of University Research Ethics Committees (URECs) owes more to the hegemonic influence of the market on the management of public sector organisations, Hedgecoe undertook two case studies – one of which involved my research into student sex work.[28] In this he used "emails, letters and minutes gathered through a Freedom of Information (FOI) request" to explore "the role of URECs in 'discouraging' this kind of research, focusing on the 2004/2005 decision by the Kingston University Faculty of Arts and Social Sciences REC regarding a proposed undergraduate research project" (Hedgecoe, 2016, p.489). The project in question was exploratory and concerned what factors influenced students' decisions to take up sex work. As the supervisor, I referred it to the Faculty Research Ethics Committee. As to what happened next, I learnt more from reading Hedgecoe's account than from my own personal involvement in the process. Consequently, I will lean heavily on that, rather than my own first-hand experience. Hedgecoe (2016, p.489–490) writes:

> To allow speedy review of the application, it was discussed via email by a subcommittee of the REC before a decision was taken at a meeting. REC members' focus was primarily on the potential risks faced by the student researcher: 'All I think we need to ascertain or build into the project is that the student carrying out the work is safe' (Anon, 2004a). Another member 'agree[s] with [name redacted] that the main issue is the safety of the student conducting the experiment. As it is [it is] not clear where the interviews/data collection will take place, except that it will be all over London and vary from person to person' (Anon, 2004b). The proposed solution to the issue of researcher safety was 'that the interviews should take place in an (public?) environment that will be safe for both the student and interviewee' and that in addition '[t]he identity of the interviewee must be kept anonymous at all times in the course of the study'. (Anon, 2004c)

This last member is relaxed enough about this proposed research to note that:

> Normally the ethics committee we [sic] would expect to see the consent form and interview schedule to check out how the project is represented to participants and the appropriateness of questions to be asked. *I'm happy to leave the final judgement here to the supervisor if the rest of the committee are [too,] in the interests of speed*...In principle then, I'm happy for the research to go ahead, but would like reassurance on the above points before the project is finally approved. (Anon, 2004c, emphasis added)

As Hedgecoe remarks, the REC at this juncture has given the impression that the project was largely unproblematic with the main ethical issue being the safety of the researcher, a person who it should be noted had been trained in self-defence. The committee meeting eventually took place and I was sent a letter noting that, "After some discussion and assurances that no harm can come to the interviewer and that potential harm to the interviewees is minimized, this project was cleared."

Alas it did not end there. The REC met again and imposed a new requirement (I quote again from Hedgecoe): "that it was '[i]mportant to ensure students from Kingston are not included'".

This effectively KO'd the intended research. Instead I undertook a different study (Roberts, et al., 2007b) – a survey, which I noted was: "'not ideal because it does not directly capture individual involvement" (although) it does have the "advantage of providing a conduit through the maze of research ethics committee Requirements'"(Roberts et al., 2007a, p.145).

Hedgecoe is up front that the material released to him under the FOI request offers no indication as to why the new requirement (that students from the university in which I was working could not be recruited into the study) was imposed. If it were possible that such a decision could be made on genuinely ethical grounds one would be forced to conclude that the students of the host university enjoyed a distinct set of human rights to those outside it – a fact which would negate the notion of universality which underpins our concept of human rights. It was obvious to me – then as now – that the condition imposed owed nothing to ethics. Hedgecoe (p.490) continues:

One obvious explanation is that Kingston University wanted to distance itself from the implication that its own students had to resort to this kind of work, and the possible resulting bad publicity...In this case, even if this was not the actual intention, the effect of the REC's final decision was, without any obvious increase in protection for research subjects, to protect the university from the potentially scandalous revelation that its students were engaged in sex work.

The analysis which Hedgecoe presents leaves the reader with a clear picture that the University Research Ethics Committee was used as "an instrument of organisational reputation management, preventing the gathering of research data" (p.490) on a topic of great public interest. In this respect, university RECs in the UK appear to function little differently from their institutional counterparts in the US – the Institutional Review Boards – which at least display a level of honesty in their stated priority to "protect institutional interests" by "weeding out politically sensitive subjects before they are approved", admitting that "academic freedom...is considered desirable but not indispensable" (cited in Hedgecoe, 2016, p.494). In the halcyon days before the ideas of Milton Friedman invaded the campus, academic freedom and protection of research participants were regarded as core principles. These seem to have been jettisoned in favour of a new one – to protect a university from reputational harm, whether real or imagined. The legal implications of this new credo will be examined later in this chapter but it is worth emphasising here that it has taken root despite it being a clear violation of Economic and Social Research Council (ESRC) guidelines which stress the necessity for ethics committees to be "free from bias and undue influence from the institution in which they are located" (ESRC, 2010, p.10).[29] One wonders if prospective committee members are informed of the ESRC's position on this.

It was not the last time research on student sex work was obstructed. I have already stated that the work published in 2015 (Roberts et al., 2015) in the journal *Sex Education* comprised a much smaller sample than originally envisaged, this being the result of a delay of several months in obtaining ethical clearance. The employment of delaying tactics to try and time out projects is a common one. Over the years I witnessed several needlessly delayed so that they could not be conducted. One of the more bizarre excuses offered for this was that the researchers would be upset by attempting to conduct focus groups with students to discuss attitudes to sex work among EU and non-EU students – and that it would be distressing for students to volunteer for focus groups in which the topic is discussed. This is in fact a clear contravention of British Psychological Society ethical guidelines which stress that participants in research should not be exposed to risks which they would not expect to encounter in real life. Since all the participants were required to do in the project was to have a conversation about a topic which has appeared in the newspapers on countless occasions, there were no risks beyond the everyday.

This infantilising of young adults at a time when the job market for them is precarious, and they are increasingly compelled to be economically dependent on others (often their families) should be envisaged as a facet of the neo-liberal project. Rather than questioning this nonsense, psychologists have been happy to play their usual role of ideologically subservient lapdog and theorise how adolescence now lasts until aged 25 (see Wallis, 2013). By such means the precariousness of the neo-liberal environment is reimagined as the vulnerable psychological state of students – a process of political projection Furedi (2016) refers to as the "weaponisation of emotion". Another excuse offered by the ethics committee was that in discussing these issues with students, the students might start discussing personal issues unconnected with the proposed research. This, of course, is a logical possibility but it is one which exists in every single research situation involving more than one person. If it is legitimate to curtail a study into students' views of sex work on these grounds then it would be legitimate to curtail all social research, no matter what the topic.

In addition to delaying tactics, I am aware of instances

where expressed objections to research have been based on an exaggerated belief in the risk of violence – an act of imagination which owes more than a little to distorted media depictions of street sex markets projected onto the entire field, with the result that sex workers become, not even the targets of violence, but the imagined source of it ready to direct it onto innocent and ill-fated researchers at the drop of a hat. Then there is the type of objection which questions the very legitimacy of research into human sexuality. As a former dean in one institution remarked: "Just why do you do this? What's the sex industry got to do with psychology?" Putting aside the fact that the said dean's speciality was English Literature, I don't think her question is addressing one of life's imponderable mysteries. When I replied that psychology was about the study of human behaviour and that that included sexual behaviour she was visibly stunned. Maybe she had never thought of this before. Perhaps the accusation that university life is too sheltered from reality has some merits I hadn't previously considered.

The examples just mentioned are far from exhaustive, but suffice to raise the possibility that individuals responsible for the decisions reached in university ethics committees may, as Hedgecoe suggests, be keeping one eye on institutional mores and the other on their own careers.[30] The subservience of research ethics to the neo-liberal imperative occurs because in the ambience of bureaucratic dread which accompanies the capitalist takeover of academia, committee members tend to see their loyalties as belonging to the institution not to the research participants, the researchers, the wider knowledge community or the public for that matter. As a result, faced with work which they know has already aroused the ire of management, they will frequently try to anticipate the intentions of those who float above them in the food chain and act to signal their own compliance with these intentions, currying favour in the hope that their obedience will be rewarded – which it may well be in this life – but surely not the next![31] Laurence Rees (2005) described a not dissimilar set of practices as characterising the chaotic workings of the Nazi government. There, they formed the backdrop to the euthanasia programme which led to the mass murder of disabled people. After the work of Stanley Milgram on obedience to authority, that this kind of second guessing of authority should occur in the present day within a psychology department of all places, suggests something seriously amiss in the way psychologists are educated or in the way the discipline is constructed or both.[32]

Image, Reputation and Academic Freedom in the Higher Education Dystopia

It's now time to consider in more depth the motives of those institutional players who are responsible for the obstruction. The abolition, or in Baudrillardian terms, the murder of the university as a state-financed educational establishment for advanced study and its replacement by a corporate simulacrum which offers degrees for huge sums of money has entailed a fundamental change in the operation of higher education institutes. In the new landscape appearances matter more than reality, brands more than product. The image is central to the brand – even if research indicates that vice-chancellors and university marketing professionals have no critical understanding of the purpose and value of branding and no evidence exists that it adds any "real value" to university life (Chapleo, 2011). Three aspects of image control help us to understand why universities seek to obstruct and discourage research into student sex work and what is at stake.

A. Image and Recruitment

Higher education managers see their primary purpose as protecting the image of the institution which they see as critical in attracting paying customers. I received the following email from the university press office following a *Sunday Times* article

(Milne, 2006) on some earlier research.

> What worries me is that although I'm sure the research does highlight it as a problem globally as well as nationally, your research is based on a survey undertaken with [our] University students and it's the publicity surrounding that which concerns me. The story has hit the international press in India which, as you probably know, is a big market for [the university]. (Roberts, 2010, p.14)

It soon became apparent that in its wish to "protect" the university, the press office had obstructed media outlets wishing to speak to me about the *Sunday Times* piece – telling all and sundry that I was not available, when I was in fact very much alive, quite healthy and in my office. Within a day I had two managers knocking on my door demanding copies of my work, not I might add to engage me in collegiate discussion about the forms of statistical analysis I had employed! All told, this was the first inkling I had that all was not right in the state of academe, that key players were paying homage to a somewhat different aesthetic than the one I had been led to believe was sacrosanct. Attempts to engage with the press office in a constructive discussion, for them to consider the research as playing a significant role in student welfare, got nowhere. What stands out in the press office's response is the direction in which concern is directed, which is not towards student welfare but towards publicity and the believed detrimental effect on recruitment that the research would have. While this is but one consequence of the globalisation of higher education markets it also betrays a fundamental ethical attitude, which is characteristic of neo-liberal regimes. By this I refer to the implied selfish stance. The research paper was abundantly clear that students' relatively recent entrance into the sex markets was an international phenomenon. Any welfare issues which arise from this are therefore also international. The anxiety on display has no truck with this and makes explicit the absence of institutional interest in a welfare perspective, whether local or beyond the borders of the university. The belief expressed by the press office is that no good can come of this knowledge. It is forbidden knowledge and as such would seem to carry a Biblical threat.

The contents of the *Sunday Times* article are of further interest because of the response elicited from Universities UK when it was approached for comment. According to the article, "A spokesman for Universities UK emphasized that the institutions provided support services for students in trouble, but 'students are responsible adults and we treat them as such'."

What we know with certainty is that universities categorically *do not* provide support services for student sex workers – the subjects who are deemed to be "in trouble". Whether students are treated as "responsible adults" – as opposed to sources of revenue – is debatable, not least because of the moral panic which arises whenever the topic of student sex work reaches even the dimmest levels of awareness in university administrators. Documents obtained through Data Protection requests in institutions in which I have worked show that the same reaction has occurred time and time again when any mention of student sex work research by academics from the university appears in the media. Except for the *SSWP* based at Swansea University – and even there the university logo is minimal or non-existent on much of the publicity material – at no point has any interest or concern with the welfare of students involved in sex work been expressed by the leaders or management of any higher education institute in the UK. Given the mantra of "enhancing the student experience" which universities regularly trot out in these dark times, the lack of interest in their welfare compared to their corporately measured satisfaction reveals the enormous gap between the universities' (commercial) rhetoric and the lived reality outside of it.

71

B. Image, Institutional Morality and the Sexual Economy of Higher Education

The sociologist Stuart Hall remarked that "the university is a critical institution or it is nothing" (cited in Giroux, 2011, p.131). If we survey the wealth of evidence from across the globe we might presently conclude that it has achieved that state of nothingness that Hall warned us about. What remains is the shop front of an academic supermarket and the festering goods on display. Everybody who has spent any appreciable time in university life knows that something is wrong. In few places, however, has self-deception been institutionalised more thoroughly than in higher education, which seemingly functions on the credo of the three wise monkeys "hear no evil, speak no evil and see no evil". The maxim is probably derived from the Confucian Analects where in Book XII, goodness is defined as "to look at nothing in defiance of ritual, to listen to nothing in defiance of ritual and to speak of nothing in defiance of ritual" (Confucius, 2000, p.153).

Confucian teachings came to serve and protect a traditional, patriarchal conservative way of life, a nostalgia for the rule of old, where "silence was golden". Now, however, is not the time to resurrect the autumn of the patriarch – or the vice-chancellor come to that! Challenging neo-liberal orthodoxy requires a deconstruction of the images and representations mass-produced in its defence and for the superficial morality which props them up to be exposed. They must be seen for what they are. Jungian psychology posits a shadow, an alternative personality waiting in the wings, poised to unmask the daily pretences and compromises that masquerade as the normal, well-adjusted life. The shadow image to the marketised university as benevolent provider of education at a price is the marketised university, parasitic on student income earned thorough labour in the libidinous industries of contemporary capitalism. This is the image of the university as latter day corporate pimp, unconcerned with the welfare of those it is financially dependent upon, thoroughly immersed in the same market dynamics as the student. These dictate survival at any price – "a slave to the sacred hunger for gold" – the "filthy lucre" which haunts respectability. This dangerous truth is part of the reason our institutions of teaching and learning seek to repress awareness and knowledge of student sex work – they do not wish to be reminded of what they see as their own moral failings – nor perhaps their own naked attachment to money and consumption – unable to acknowledge their place in what Hannah Arendt (1976, ix) referred to as "the subterranean stream of Western history". This is a topic worthy perhaps of a more thorough psychoanalytic investigation of the institution.

Other moral issues lurk in the undergrowth. The Faustian pact with the industries of marketing and public relations requires that the pillars of truth in the new corporate landscape be hidden from view. From a neo-liberal vantage point it is an unwelcome source of negative public relations. Advertising and public relations are ultimately about lies and misrepresentation. Hence, a conspiracy of public silence about the unholy principles that govern higher education necessarily prevails. They have served to gentrify corruption long before the sex industry received its own makeover in the high street leisure and entertainment industries. Respectability has always spoken with a forked tongue, dressed in a shirt and tie and backed by money and power. Of course, providing sexual services to obtain a "good education" is not a marketing dream, neither for higher education institutions nor the NUS, both of which function as business bedfellows that profit from the student body. It must also be said that the alarmist panic which greets student sex work research owes something to the wider cultural panic about sex trafficking which has been promoted by policy makers and which itself is situated in a much larger xenophobic retaliation against the free movement of migrant workers in a risky, culturally diverse changing Europe.[33]

But there is a further piece to the jigsaw which must be put in place before this picture is complete. One cannot hope to understand the nature and power of the denial, obstruction and hostility[34] which greets student sex work, nor the institutional incentives which underpin it, without considering the broader legal framework, its relation to political structures which defend wealth and how cherished notions of academic freedom fare under it.

C. Image, Reputation and Law

A long-standing and cherished notion is that the activities of academic staff are protected under the mantel of academic freedom. For example, the United Nations Educational Scientific and Cultural Organisation has recommended (UNESCO, 1997) that "the principle of academic freedom should be scrupulously observed". The UK is a signatory to this recommendation and its own Education Reform Act (1988, section 202) supposedly enshrines the legal right of academics[35] "to question and test received wisdom and to put forward new ideas and controversial or unpopular opinions without placing themselves in jeopardy of losing their jobs or the privileges they may have".

Closely related to the notion of academic freedom is the right to freedom of expression as afforded by Article 10 of the European Convention on Human Rights (ECHR, 1998) in the first clause of which it is stated: "Everyone has the right to freedom of expression. This right shall include freedom to hold opinions and to receive and impart information and ideas without interference by public authority and regardless of frontiers."

At face value, the quote provided earlier from a higher education manager (Roberts, 2010, p.15) that a "chosen line of research" – in this case student sex work – will have "consequences in terms of future employability" and that I "must compromise... academic freedom" would appear to demonstrate a clear breach of this, indeed the wording of the 1988 act and the managerial threat appear incompatible by any reasonable interpretation of what either expression is meant to convey. Despite the presence of the Education Reform Act and the European Convention on Human Rights, concerns have arisen following the outcome of two recent cases in the UK. Greatorex (2013a) describes the first of these:

> ...in Hill v Great Tey Primary School UKEAT/0237/12/SM, a dinner lady who told a child's parents that their daughter had been tied to a fence and whipped with a skipping rope by some other pupils, and subsequently repeated that to the press. These allegations were true, but the dinner lady was dismissed for breach of confidentiality and acting in a manner likely to bring the school into disrepute. Lawyers for the dinner lady argued that this represented an unjustified interference with her right to freedom of speech under Art 10 of the ECHR.
>
> The EAT (Langstaff J presiding) rejected this argument, holding that a school had a reputation to protect, and that it was entitled to take steps to manage the flow of information from a school in the interests of all pupils and staff... Though we consider that the disciplinary proceedings constituted a restriction upon the claimant's freedom of speech, it was open to the school to seek to justify the interference by reference to the legitimate aims of protecting the reputation.

The Employment Appeals Tribunal (EAT) here is in effect drawing on the second clause of Article 10 (emphasis in bold below) which places restrictions on the context in which freedoms may be exercised.[36] That is, the exercise of freedom of expression under the article is a "qualified right" only.

The exercise of these freedoms, since it carries with it duties and responsibilities, may be subject to such formalities, conditions, restrictions or penalties as are prescribed by law and are necessary in a democratic society, in the interests of national security, territorial integrity or public safety, for the prevention of disorder or crime, for the protection of health or morals, **for the protection of the reputation or rights of others**, for preventing the disclosure of information received in confidence, or for maintaining the authority and impartiality of the judiciary.

A second case – Duke v University of Salford [2013] EWHC 196 (QB) – also discussed by Greatorex (2013b), describes how the UK High Court confirmed that a university is also entitled to protect its reputation by suing in defamation.[37] What both these cases illustrate is that educational institutions, including universities, are in a class which entitles them to protect their reputation – this being the case because they are held to be organisations which "are in competition to secure funding by admitting pupils" and, of course, students (Greatorex, 2013a). Effectively, interpretation of the law functions to protect private corporations and institutions so that, as is true of so much else in contemporary society, structures, processes and procedures are designed or deformed to preserve power, privilege and concentrated wealth. At face value, this would appear to protect institutions against potential revelations of any kind of scandalous practice – including financial malfeasance. In the circumstances, it is not surprising that UK academics believe that the levels of academic freedom they enjoy are among the poorest in Europe (UCU, 2017). Research by Karran and Mallinson (2017) lends support to this. Their analysis of 37 different legislative elements, using a composite measure of legal protection for academic freedom (teaching, research, institutional autonomy, self-governance, academic tenure and adherence to international agreements) put the UK second to the bottom of the list of EU nation states.

Farrington and Palfreyman (2012) duly commented that with regards to "the health of academic freedom, the UK is clearly the sick man of Europe".

The current legal interpretations which effectively disregard the right to academic freedom in favour of the maintenance of corporate image should then be considered an aspect of what Winters (2011, p.9) refers to as "the politics of wealth defense" by materially endowed actors. Braben's (2008) comment that academic freedom was now "too costly a commodity to be distributed widely" seems unerringly near the truth. As the diktats of corporate image and branding occupy a revered place in the UK higher education landscape and the dominant philosophy of governance equates to a type of managerial fundamentalism, the hope that the academic community can function as a dependable source of critical insight into the nature of the world we inhabit may already have passed into history.

In the next chapter, I will extend the present analysis into the disciplinary practices of the university with a consideration of the essential place of psychological governance in the furtherance of neo-liberalism and how this is not simply a stratagem for the subjugation of the rebellious mind but an extensive project to tame and discipline the physical bodies of the wild citizens who hold out the prospects of a different future.

The concluding chapter will be a re-imagining of that future and the role of education in political resistance.

The offing was barred by a black bank of clouds, and the tranquil waterway leading to the uttermost ends of the earth flowed sombre under an overcast sky – seemed to lead into the heart of an immense darkness
Joseph Conrad 2012, p.89

Chapter Four

Psycho-Politics and the Body Politic: The University and the State

Psychological governance is compulsory, unthinking and potentially repressive
Eccleston, 2017, p.71.

the doors of the magic theatre...had promised so many wonderful things
Hesse, 2012, p.228.

The neo-liberal project can be understood primarily as the latest incarnation of political economic hegemony by ruling elites. Since the advent of capitalism, each new period of its domination has shaped an appropriate psychological receptivity to its requirements – a mass acceptance of the limited "horizons of possibility" (Fisher, 2009, p.2009) bequeathed by the status quo in relations of power, prestige and justice. This "capitalist realism" as Mark Fisher described it, has taken a peculiar turn in neo-liberalism.

Critics are cognisant that automation has attained levels of sophistication beyond compare – predicted to reach an apotheosis in the near future with the emergence of genuine non-biological intelligence – a point in our technological, cultural and biological evolution which Kurzweil (2005) has termed the "singularity". The arrival on the human scene of machine consciousness will be a consequence and culmination of an economic imperative which has driven development since the mid-eighteenth century. Yet there is a paradox about this envisaged high point in the mechanisation of production in that the journey to artificial intelligence has been fuelled by an increasing reliance on forms of human subjectivity conducive to the illusion of perpetual economic growth. The birth of cybernetic consciousness will thus depend on the manifestation of a very particular mode of human consciousness, a subjectivity nurtured by capital.

The cultivation of the post-industrial landscape has led to a spectacular dependence not just on human emotional labour but on forms of psychological governance which seek to mould, configure, influence and control the cognitive and affective contours of human life.[38] Psychology, for so long an accomplice to capitalism, has, under neo-liberalism, seen its language decoupled from the discipline and appropriated by states and corporations jockeying for position amid the global turmoil of the early twenty-first century. With little critical attention, "psychological vulnerability" has become the battleground between critical forces seeking to ameliorate the brutal consequences of neo-liberalism, and state and corporate forces seeking to impose and prioritise that vulnerability as a condition of control. The similarity of discursive referents on both sides – well-being, social justice, mental health signals a moment of extreme danger. If the left does not develop a radical critique of how constructions of mental health – notably diagnoses and labelling – whether by self or other, function in a wider politics of consciousness, then the risk is that its actions will give substance and nourishment to the very forces which promote the existential (psychiatric) categories that it needs to overthrow. Internalising identities of fragility and weaponising emotions rather than cultivating forms of support which build resilience is a risky ploy.[39] Wearing a badge of "mental health system survivor" is a more effective and empowering rhetorical resource than the identity of being "mentally ill". While it does not avoid connotations of vulnerability – which after all is part of the human condition – it does avoid expressing that vulnerability as a lack, a persistent and enduring "deficit" which exists inside oneself, absorbing responsibility for all the social, economic and political sins of the world. It is not surprising that it is the latter "deficit model" which is flourishing on campus, as the cultural remit becomes one of pleasing and placating students rather than challenging them. Such "therapeutic education" creates, Eccleston and Hayes (2009) write, "A diminished image of human potential [which] opens up people's emotions to assessment by the state and encourages dependence on ritualised forms of emotional support offered by state agencies...[It] replaces education with the social engineering of emotionally literate citizens who are also coached to experience emotional well-being."

Ideas of what constitutes emotional well-being are assumed rather than discussed. Protest, justifiable anger and outrage, it may be added, rarely feature in them, nor in organisational and state prescriptions of the happy citizen. The growth in mental health problems in young people in recent years is better understood, not as an index of personal failure but as a consequence of the brutal economic circumstances which have seen cuts in investment, training and job opportunities for young people, low wages, exorbitant student loans and tuition fees, cuts to mental health and welfare services, as well as a savage primary and secondary school system where endemic testing has become the norm.[40] To these multiple failures to invest in young people can be added the normalisation of exploitative advertising and marketing which uses the bodies and images of young people to sell them dreams of unattainable lifestyles, property and wealth. The higher education industry is a net contributor to this conveyor belt of impossible aspirations.

The Therapeutic State

Thomas Szasz, the libertarian psychiatrist, is best known for his seminal critique of the biological underpinnings of mental health, *The myth of mental illness* (Szasz, 1960, 1961), and his attacks on the legitimacy of psychiatric authority. Szasz railed against legally sanctioned bureaucratic politic power operating under the guise of medicine and health care, and ably supported by the power of Big Pharma to threaten, at once, our ideals of democratic freedoms and personal responsibility. In the therapeutic state, the right to freedom is overridden by the right of the state to diagnose, treat and legally sanction, in the name of health care, behaviours and states of mind which it deems undesirable to the body politic. The therapeutic state in Szasz's terms creates hopelessness and lack of responsibility and intensifies vulnerability.

Szasz's criticism of psychiatric power has been applauded on the left. However, his admonitions against the "therapeutic state" (Szasz, 2001, 2002), with its merging of psychiatric and state power on the one hand and private and public health on the other, have been less well received. Confusion about Szasz's work has arisen through the quite different political cultures within which it has been interpreted, even by those who oppose institutional psychiatry in its current incarnation. His work has been claimed and repudiated by those on both the left and right – deemed a liberal in some quarters and a fascist in others – with the claims and counterclaims rooted in the predilections of the critics for different configurations of state power. European intellectual tradition on the left, for example – with few exceptions – maintains a belief and a desire that state power can be harnessed for the good.[41] Szasz, a native Hungarian Jewish refugee from both Nazism and Stalinism, remained sceptical of this idea, seeing the state as fundamentally coercive and its operations predisposed to malevolent rather than benevolent outcomes.

A familiarity with Szasz's concerns regarding the corporate therapeutic state is a useful preparation for understanding our present predicament. Foucault's concerns with the biopolitics of disciplinary regimes is another. Indeed, Foucault's own position has been described by some commentators as both anti-statist and at times supportive of neo-liberalism (Zamora and Behrent, 2016). What this suggests is that considerable room still exists on the left for a rethinking of the purpose of the state alongside the age-old problematic of the relationship between individual freedoms and state structures/political governance. To envisage neo-liberalism as the only solution to this dilemma demonstrates nothing but a lack of imagination. One result of the left's consistent failure to articulate alternatives for social transformation outside of the remit of state power has been that ideas critical of it have been easily assimilated under the rubric of neo-liberalism. As neo-liberalism weakens, other possibilities are likely to present themselves. Local community initiatives, for example in food production, transport, mutual social support, education and skills exchange, may be key to expanding the space where forms of collective public action rather than state power or individual choice are sovereign.

In the neo-liberal assault on both the state and individual freedoms we see unanticipated refractions and inversions of this dialectic – witness the movement into identity politics as the point of departure for political action in tandem with the apparent reduced freedom of the state to act outside of the strictures of international capital. The rise of identity politics sees the individual as a singular actor reconfigured as a source of multiple structured and overlapping identities, any one of which may be the seat of political engagement, while the corporate nemesis (here the university or the state) is characterised by its absence of freedom – an absence which terrorises the campus in the accelerating parasitic interests of the impersonal busybody state (Appleton, 2016).[42] Each side has been invaded by its corresponding previously submerged alterity (structure and servitude respectively; individual identity reflects the structures of the social world and the corporate university acts in servitude to capitalism) to reveal, in their mutual antagonistic relations, the Kafkaesque dread of the empty throne. Nobody is in charge in an escalating de-centred theatre of the absurd, no angel of liberation to rescue the fate of humanity. Foucault, acknowledging this absence of transcendent authority, posited an agentless discourse as a driving force of history, albeit one whose absent origins and lack of purpose offers no instinctive alliance to the historical project of emancipation.[43] Foucault interprets the history of revolutionary struggle through the lens of acquiring power, not of achieving justice.[44] He proclaimed at various times the "death of the author" and the "death of man". Where this leaves a history of anything – as history is always made and told by human beings about human beings – is a problem which the left has been happy to overlook in its commandeering of Foucault's exposition of disciplinary power, knowledge, madness and sexuality. While Copernicus, Galileo, Marx and Freud can be said to have removed humanity from the centre stage, Foucault would have it that we have no place in the theatre at all. This tension, between private citizen and public/corporate state, returned with a vengeance in the UK's referendum on EU membership. It remains taut. The diminution of US global power, the rise of China and return of Russia to great power status further exacerbates the uncertainties over which forms of governance and citizenship will endure. The ongoing instability means everything is contestable – and in this form of predictable unpredictability capitalism has created one of the conditions for its own radical restructuring, if not imminent demise. Changes in the higher education landscape then need to be viewed against this larger backdrop – one suffused with the imprint of human vulnerability (existential, political and economic) throughout the civic and political order; anxieties in the edifice of personal identity echoing the unrelenting often hidden anxieties of elites in the face of a crumbling socio-political order. The rise of the therapeutic state is arguably a last throw of the dice to heal a misaligned, misfiring, misanthropic and dysfunctional polity. Just as "mental illness" is a literary device run riot, confusing the metaphor of bodily illness for real "disease" in the mind, so too with the therapeutic state – where what needs to be corrected in the management of the state is not the psycho-emotional condition of the people who inhabit it but the very system of governance itself.

Psychology has been a willing accomplice in the privatisation of stress (Fisher, 2009, 2017) supplementing the neo-liberal destruction of the welfare state with an enforced diet of positive thinking, psychotherapy, counselling, CBT and mindfulness. Organised political action and how to cultivate it surprisingly failed to appear on its inventory of panaceas to life's troubles.

With that, we can now turn to examine various other forms of subjectivity – the subject positions – which permeate life on the campus – both those which fortify the corporate university acting on behalf of the neo-liberal state and those which challenge and resist it.

Subjectivity in Obedience

Occupying pride of place among the compliant, market-disciplined modes of subjectification on parade at university central is the student as consumer. This consumer endorses education as a desirable commodity, available at a price, which when purchased comes with the undesirable "free gift" of a pre-packaged emotional vulnerability to the stresses of the neo-liberal system.[45] A case of *caveat emptor*.[46] This vulnerability includes a necessary fear of the (financial and occupational) future, which in its public expression is reinterpreted as the manifestation of a personality deficit. Next, there is the mathematically engineered "satisfied student" – the happy citizen operationally brought into being through participation in the NSS. As we have already dismissed the measures which arise from the NSS as valid indicators of quality of education, it is time to consider what exactly they do denote.

We saw in chapter one that from students' point of view,

"satisfaction" marks the confidence with which they face the labour market – an indicator of how they anticipate their future in the world of work. A further possibility, scarcely imagined, is that students assign scores in line with what they think is the reputation of the institution in the eyes of others – the significant others being either the media or friends studying in other institutions varying in prestige. These social representations of university status have largely escaped scrutiny, though they may be crucial to understanding the bigger picture. A broader and not unrelated perspective is that NSS scores simply function as a proxy for the perceived financial health of the institution. For example, Coventry University's elevation to 11th place in the 2016 rankings and 15th place in *The Guardian* league tables of the same year – the highest ever places for a former polytechnic – followed a massive investment programme in infrastructure and the lowering of staff-student ratios to one of the most favourable in the country. These factors can be considered distinct from the socio-economic background or financial well-being of the students themselves and the expectations they bring with them. Figures from 2017 indicate that 84 per cent of students report that they "feel happy with the quality of their education" (Pells, 2017a). If we take the government's perspective, this figure shows that an awful lot of students are happy with what they are getting. If we factor in the response rate, which is around 68 per cent, this actually suggests a somewhat reduced figure for those satisfied (57 per cent). If, however, we were to factor in reality and a wider knowledge of what education could be like, the truer figure may be considerably lower.[47]

What we see in the use of league tables is an ideological commitment to dressing up the material and economic resources of an institution (which includes the social, cultural and material capital of its students) in the clothes of a psychological propensity purportedly possessed by its students – an index of sorts of their affective orientation towards their place of study. A similar conjuring trick has taken place with school league tables. There, explanations of students' performance in examinations, something strongly influenced by structural inequalities (for example, the socio-economic characteristics of the geographic area/neighbourhood in which a school is situated, whose origins lie far outside the school gates – see Goodman, Sibieta and Washbrook, 2009; Connelly, Sullivan and Jerrim, 2014; Morris, Dorling and Davey Smith, 2016), are instead posited in terms of pupil characteristics, family background or school characteristics. The latter parameter is one which parents can inspect, when exercising their alienated "free choice" over where to send their children. This practice reproduces an illusion of the choice exercised by wealthy parents over which private school they should send their children to. Although the practice of rank ordering schools has been criticised as unhelpful, misleading and unfit for purpose by members of The Royal Statistical Society (Goldstein and Leckie, 2008; Bird et al., 2005) – a failed but valiant attempt to buttress ideology with reason – the rankings are still promoted as a vehicle for "consumer" choice and likewise with university league tables. If a child subsequently fails to succeed educationally, this is then explained away as the results of poor parental choice, lack of motivation or lack of ability (or indeed all three) on the part of the student. The underlying policy preoccupation, as Gillies and Edwards (2017, p112) tell us, is but, "The latest incarnation of a long-standing conviction held by the rich and powerful – specifically, that there must be something inherently wrong with the minds, bodies and souls of those failing to thrive in an unfettered free market economy."

In the cruel fantasy of the right, inequality is a lifestyle choice, as is the suffering which goes with it. The market must remain, and reign, supreme, helped along by an ingrained psychological subservience which accepts it as natural or pre-ordained.

The tactic of placing student "satisfaction" at the centre of the UK government's coercive transformation of higher education reflects a regression to simpler views of human nature. Jeremy Bentham's claim that the contours of human motivation forever lie between the "sovereign masters" of pleasure and pain seems a suitable frame for the government's aim of forcing universities to maximise the "satisfaction" – for which read, happiness or pleasure – of its students or else face the punitive consequences of reduced funding. Together with the Social Darwinist undertones of the league tables, this reads as a modern governmental espousal of behaviourism – the philosophy advocated by B.F. Skinner – which promised a utopia "beyond freedom and dignity". A crucial difference, however, is that whereas Skinner envisaged the good life emerging from an administrative manipulation of individuals' reinforcement histories, the government prescribes reinforcement at an institutional level – where a move up the league tables (or improved NSS scores) is akin to positive reinforcement, and a move in the opposite direction akin to punishment. The universities dutifully swim in this disciplinary tide.

Foucault described discipline as a "political technology of the body" (cited in Rabinow, 1991, p.171). In the present context, this is apt if one conceives of the body in much wider terms than the singular corpus of the indebted, fearful student. The university looks Janus-faced upon the world, an institution of discipline and a disciplined institution, a part being self-discipline. Hence the multiplication of bureaucracy, the total output of which, across the sector, leads to an institutional beauty contest where universities boast of their pointless successes in the hope of convincing themselves, their students and the wider public that all is well, in the best of all possible worlds.[48] Few outside the chancellery appear convinced. In deference to government strictures, the policy orientation of universities has drifted towards the manufacture of neo-liberal mood states on campus – in staff as much as students – with the staff being as easily hypnotised by journal impact factors and REF ratings as students are by NSS scores – perhaps more so. Parker (2014) has described how the marketisation of higher education has intensified pressure on female middle management to ameliorate discontent induced by neo-liberal policies in the workplace. To do this they turn to their repertoires of emotional labour. The "feminisation" of middle management has in this way operated as a buffer zone not only to protect senior management from the anger stirred up below but to force through unpopular management decisions in the name of institutional loyalty. In a similar vein, the emotional labour exerted by female management finds its parallel in staff efforts to present a united front to students that all is well, when the reality is somewhat different. This recourse to feminine emotional labour as a key piece in the management jigsaw reveals yet a further way in which universities run in a parallel fashion to the sex industry.

It is the body of students as a collective, however, which must be constrained to reproduce compliant cognitive and affective appraisals of their host institution, and the body of staff which must act in a manner to convince them that the game is meaningful and for real. What the campus apparatchiks do not understand is that tables of numbers produced through torturous bureaucratic means seldom excite affective responses – other than those of boredom, futility and disbelief – in those exposed to them. Followers of the industrial production figures which were routinely disseminated by the Soviet regime know this well. As totalising bureaucracy lays waste to one's sense of reality, humour becomes an essential tool – a means to survive by "resisting structure". Svetlana Boym (1994, p.289) referred to such resistance as the "central structuring principle of Soviet life". Unfortunately, the NSS has yet to become a subject of mirth – which is a pity as it is widely described as a joke!

The "satisfaction" reproduced by the NSS is like the satisfaction produced by the USSR – not real satisfaction at all – not in the sense of denoting the "fulfilment of one's wishes, expectations or needs, or the pleasure derived from this". The universities' "pleasure principle" is an officially sanctioned lie, another feature of the looking-glass world simultaneously accepted and denied in the manner of most totalitarian pronouncements – not entirely believed even by the perpetrators. Students' acquiescence to assessments of "satisfaction" can therefore best be understood as another form of emotional labour, wrought under duress from the hapless students. They little realise that their compliance aids the production of an impoverished form of education that they are condemned to "experience" and for which they must pay through the nose.

As currently understood, the focus on "experience" and "satisfaction" leads to an arms race towards the subterranean depths of dark education. Staff, held responsible for their students' "progress" – by which is meant not success but failure, must work to ensure their students are content, rather than intellectually challenged. A *folie* à *deux*, a tango of emotional labour, ensues in which: "lecturers are put under pressure to cut reading lists and shorten assessments. If students do not like reading whole books, then perhaps extracts will do. If they find essay-writing difficult, then lecturers should guide them step-by-step through what to write and how, rather than leaving them to work it out for themselves. If students do not like exams, then maybe a poster would suffice" (Williams, 2015).

Lest this be thought an exaggeration, let me say at once that it is not; I was regularly confronted with students who let me know, with some insistence as well as surprise, that they had been explicitly instructed by other staff not to read books! In such an environment, the library ceases to be a library at all and the books on its shelves become nothing more than ghostly reminders of past social and intellectual possibilities, a museum of traditions threatening to escape the bonds of remembrance. In Calvino's (1997) *Invisible Cities*, "desires are already memories". In the university library, memories have ceased to be desires;

the loveless books with their unread chapters another essay in the slow death of the university and the impending cancellation of the future. Once the centrepiece of the liberal world, the university has been reduced to an external appearance, a hollowed-out reminder of an ideal pursued through centuries. This appearance also resembles a front for organised crime – which in a way is exactly what the murder of reality is. And like other institutions which have proclaimed and flaunted their liberal credentials – and I have in mind here sections of the mainstream media – an unquestioning reactionary agenda on mental health is invariably found when the desideratum is to manage the conduct of potentially uncooperative free agents. For the modern university, those troublesome agents are students; for the media, unruly viewers, listeners and readers. They must be kept in check, less thoughtcrime exceed tolerable limits.

Although the university has been progressively and thoroughly immersed in therapeutic culture, the usual tools of that culture – drugs, psychotherapy, mindfulness and positive thinking – are not equally accessible for tactical deployment. With drug prescribing legally restricted to medical professionals and psychotherapy expensive and in short supply, the instrument of choice is "positive thinking". Thus happiness (in the guise of student satisfaction) is compulsory, aided and abetted by government coercion, an obedient administrative class and media collusion. The corporate version of unhappiness, operationally defined as lower than expected student satisfaction, is not something which can be bolstered by collective political action, unlike the real-world version. The abolition of loans, the re-introduction of maintenance grants, improvements in pay and conditions in work – political measures which would require a collective will and action to realise – would do wonders to reduce the widespread misery among the student population. Students as a political force must therefore reject the neo-liberal model which seeks to privatise stress and impose upon them, in psychological form, the burdens of a failed system of governance. Rejecting this requires they give up the pseudo-political individual power to make their education easier in the form of better grades and less challenging assignments. That is, students as well as staff must decide what the university is for.

Dissident Subjectivities

Foucault argued that subjects are made by power – that one's subjective orientation to the world is constituted by the confrontation with power – which itself sets the parameters on what is known. Not all subjectivities enabled by regimes of power, however, are convenient to its smooth operation, even if they stand in its shadow. Alongside the positions cultivated to uphold the status quo are those which the students themselves have nurtured as means for their own defence. Foucault believed that it is through revolt that subjectivity is brought into history (see Gutting, 2005, p.30). Revolt has long been a feature of the history of subjectification and sexual relations have often occupied a prominent place in that history. The sex workers' rights movement is a new chapter in it.

The decision of students to participate in sex work is a direct consequence of the corporate makeover of higher education and a direct consequence of the turn to psychological governance – that social and economic life ought to be led by the endless search for leisure and pleasure. As we have seen, the students who have taken this decision are considered to have transgressed the moral and social boundaries considered normative by campus management while the moral transgressions associated with various forms of administrative corruption have invited neither punitive responses nor denigration. The only organised response common to both groups' actions is literal denial – a specific form of denial which Stanley Cohen (2001, p.104) thought characteristic of authoritarian and repressive regimes – free to operate in environments "lacking domestic accountability and insulated from external scrutiny". Cohen further observed that there are no limits to the methods used to explain away or deny the most obvious of realities. Thus, we can expect this denial to continue. But what we can deduce from this is that the subjective position occupied by student sex workers is a political rather than a moral one and hence it is a political critique of the situation that is required not a moral one. This conclusion gains traction from the fact that student sex workers, as the offspring of neo-liberal education, have adopted the same entrepreneurial spirit and attitude to capital accumulation and investment as the institutions in which they are housed. Whether sexual capital or finance capital, in neo-liberalism, it's the same game – to "configure all aspects of existence in economic terms" (Wendy Brown cited in Rhodes, 2017). Their disciplined body is the same disciplined body possessed by all academic staff and all students. The real body in question is the one patrolled by capitalist real-politic not the one utilised for gain in the sex markets.

The punitive measures which student sex workers potentially face from universities ought to be seen then not as rational responses to transgressions of accepted moral codes but as disciplinary threats directed at what students – and it is worth emphasising that we are talking here about predominantly female students – choose to do with their bodies in violation of the wishes of predominantly white male managers. It is an inherited disciplinary regime directed at controlling and regulating the manner in which female students choose to exercise their sexuality. Whether students engage in sexual labour is not by its nature something easily subjected to direct surveillance (unlike the disciplinary regimes directed towards mental compliance; the NSS, REF, TEF and so on). This is something it has in common with many other types of employment which entail commodified intimate "body work" – for example beauty work, massage, nursing and forms of health and social care.[49] The university is not yet a prison – even if academic staff might feel it is heading in that direction. Student sex work then is feared, not just because it threatens the illusion of purity emanating from the sanctimonious corporate brand but because it threatens to expose that purity and its accompanying prurience as illusion and with it the unholy nature of the corporate beast. In addition, it functions as a threat to the limits of power that can be exerted by the neo-liberal university and beyond that the state. They resist ideological assimilation and incorporation into the disciplinary status quo. While disciplinary power continues to produce staff redundancies; dismissals; threats to employment; bureaucratic compliance in course delivery, research administration and the content of research work – not to mention the manufacture of neo-liberal mood states to support the aforementioned – students continue to participate in the global sex markets irrespective of the opprobrium they risk.

In Scambler's (2007) typology of sex workers, students might be classed as opportunists, driven by the economic need to finance their studies, time-limited travellers in the business of flogging erotic labour.[50] Unlike the more compliant psychological orientations fashioned by the neo-liberal university, however, the path taken by student sex workers to meet their needs is greeted with disdain by those in charge of the corporate "mission". These students therefore embody a paradox at the heart of capitalism. Even as they internalise its logic and exchange erotic services for remuneration, they refuse its judgement and in so doing strike a double blow at the beating heart of the capitalist university – undermining the public relations department's efforts to promote brand image while exposing the insincere claims of the sector to be beholden to the interests and well-being of students. One may surmise from this that truth destroys illusory image and that the citadel of capitalist realism is not guarded on all fronts. But there is also a deeper, distinctly Nietzschean lesson residing in this. In *Twilight of the Idols,* Nietzsche (1968) provides a brief sketch of the history of metaphysics, in the concluding section of which he surmises that the real and true world is no longer an idea of any use, but that in its abolition the apparent world is also destroyed.[51] Under late capitalism the real and apparent have merged into one – the world to which we are told there is no alternative. But if there *really* were no alternative would we need to be told so? In Lacanian terms, we might say that the domain of the real lies beyond the symbolic and the imaginary. Unknowable, it can be brought into being – *realised* – only by action. What is left from these ruins is for us to give new meaning to life – to reclaim ordinary happiness and misery from the clutches of the bean counters and pen pushers who feed off their reconstructed corporate imaginings; a difficult enough undertaking with behavioural science's complicity in capitalism.

The actions of this marginalised group of students expose a flaw in the edifice of the neo-liberal university. Paradoxes and contradictions in capitalism are fractures in its ideological superstructure. The task is to widen the cracks, to open windows onto other worlds. If the primary duty for this was apportioned to the working class in nineteenth- and twentieth-century politics, we must recognise that in the twenty-first century the necessary agents are more widely distributed and that power may lie in unforeseen places and in hitherto unrealised connections. If the second half of the twentieth century undermined the claims of the proletariat to be the vanguard revolutionary class, this does not mean that we should view identity politics as a retreat from necessary struggle. Intersectionality has taken its place in the language of the new left. As Parker (2017) has argued, it enables a necessary questioning of the disconnect between class politics and other forms of struggle and opens up new opportunities for alliance, for co-creation, for mutual identification, for appraising the world and deciding where and how we are going to reconfigure it.

The pervading discourse in society in which women are construed as dangerous and in need of control is long standing.

It is the early seventeenth century before the criminalisation of women for "night walking" begins to outpace the arrest of men for the same activity: that is, their simple physical presence on the street during the hours of darkness. This was an activity which irrespective of gender had been considered "lewd", "idle" and "vagrant" (Beaumont, 2015). This regulation of women – particularly single women – and what they do when the sun goes down begins prior to the introduction of urban street lighting. The discourse we have inherited from this "unenlightened" period and its subsequent refraction through Victorian times remains trapped in a primitive fear of darkness, disorder and disease. Then and now, fear of the corrupting influence of sex workers was in part a concern with the effect they might have on the rich; then "susceptible" gentlemen and now the wealthy university. In the contemporary denial and obstruction perpetrated by university leaders we see the same general pattern. The university and its public commitment to rationalism ought to be the place where the subject of sexual labour could be brought into the light. Alas, the legal and policy agenda which has evolved, rooted in this archaic discourse – one of control, constrain and contain – has paid little heed to what research has revealed about the practicalities of sexual labour in its various and numerous forms (Sanders and Campbell, 2014). As a result, political interest in the safety and well-being of sex workers remains, while not non-existent, certainly muted.

The radical potential for sex workers to build alliances with other constituencies against the corporate university is offset by their political (and therefore public) isolation and stigmatised identity. Current debates revolve around the nature of sexual-service provision as a form of work and the relationship of sex work to migration, coercion, law enforcement and feminism. This is not the place to rekindle these debates, which it is fair to say have often been heated – not least by the contemporary political climate in which fear of the "other" looms large. It is a fear which brings with it an obstinate refusal to listen to the women who are the supposed subjects of concern. However, it is worth stressing that the emotional legacy of a centuries old discourse which has surrounded women who sell sex persists throughout much of what passes for contemporary opinion. The potential for student sex work to inform a wider agenda of resistance and broaden the public space in which sex work is considered will be gauged by the extent to which a resurgent feminist consciousness on campus is able to tie the issue of sex work (and its accompanying neo-liberal conditions of labour, self-reflexivity and body management) to the broader one of female mistreatment there.[52] Evidence from both the US and UK points to an alarming level of sexual violence against female students; one of the largest studies conducted in the US estimated that 19 per cent, or almost one in five college women, had experienced sexual assault during their studies (Krebs at al., 2007) while data from the UK has put the figure at 34 per cent or approximately one in three (Goldhill and Bingham, 2015). The UK figures are rendered more disturbing by suggestions that higher education institutions are shirking their legal responsibility to investigate sexual assault allegations. I am aware of one institution where, at the time of writing, there are 18 concurrent allegations of sexual assault being quietly directed to the hinterlands by university authorities. A recent case in the UK concerning the physical assault of a female student at Sussex University (Pells, 2017b; Turner, 2017) is an instructive example of how university management prioritises silence and image reputation over students' well-being.

Dr Lee Salter, a lecturer in Media and Communications at that university, was arrested for assaulting a student with whom he had been in a relationship. Salter punched and stamped on the student as well as pouring salt into her eyes and ears. He was subsequently found guilty of assault and criminal damage. Despite the protests of the student, Salter continued in his teaching post for 10 months after his arrest. Only after *The Independent* newspaper raised the case did the university open disciplinary proceedings. A subsequent independent investigation conducted by Professor Nicole Westmarland, a leading researcher on domestic violence from Durham University, criticised the HR department for prioritising the protection of the attacker and the university's reputation over student safety.[53] The case, she wrote, was far from being "an isolated occurrence". On reviewing further reports brought to her attention, Westmarland found that "the abuse and harassment was linked to sex, gender identity, sexuality or disability, and that a common theme was that victims felt the university's prime concern appeared to be to make excuses as to why the alleged perpetrator acted in such a way".

Westmarland made several recommendations and a mealy-mouthed apology was eventually wrought from the vice-chancellor's lips. However, it is evident that without media involvement little or nothing would have been done; students would have remained at risk and the university would have sailed on into the academic night, blown by the prevailing winds of PR, proud of its reputation in gender studies and proclaiming how marvellously "satisfied" its students were.

The neo-liberal mood remains steadfast in university life, not solely because of government enforcement but because of willing accomplices on site and the absence of any concerted viable resistance. Questions need to be asked as to why the resistance has been so feeble. It is too simple to say that staff and students have been cowed into submission, too afraid to do anything but raise the white flag. Fear is, of course, part of the overall picture but it is also undeniably true that other factors play a substantial role. A serious impediment to opposing neo-liberalism on campus remains the time-limited nature of students' tenure there. In principle, this could be countered in two ways. First, by developing long-term political and educational programmes which aim at fostering a political identity for students and second, by forging stronger links with the one group whose presence is not so time limited – the academic staff. Serious planning and deliberation – geared towards ensuring non-cooperation with the neo-liberal agenda – needs to be structurally embedded into the heart of the NUS's mission. Who within it knows anything of its history – its past successes and failures and the lessons to be drawn from them? These are matters of education and its transmission to future generations that have an essential place in educational politics.

It must also be said that the NUS's task is made more difficult by the weak opposition coming from the academics' own union (UCU). Bailey and Freedman's (2011) *Manifesto for Resistance* carried an impressive list of individual signatories in favour of its demands for changing higher education – which were cogent, realisable, bold and radical. Unfortunately, there is no sign of it having received any organisational backing from the UCU. The union's practical concerns continue to revolve around pensions, job security and salaries – all worthy endeavours – but the absence of any strategic and ongoing opposition to the neo-liberal takeover of higher education and its enforced transformation of the bona fide business of the university (teaching and research) into a bureaucratic and market-friendly monster is problematic. There has been no consistent or vociferous opposition to any of the market indices (TQA, RAE/REF, TEF, NSS) brought in to discipline higher education and the union's own policy hub makes no mention of any of these or the corporate makeover of higher education more generally.[54]

Two significant issues must be recognised and addressed. Neither will be easy. First is the tendency for union representatives to be co-opted into management interests. For the management, promotion of weaker academics to more senior positions than their academic output warrants is a simple means of getting local union officials on message. Second and a more significant issue, because it is structural rather than haphazard, is the fact that the

UCU continues to represent two categories of staff – the main body of academic staff and the management – groups which have fundamentally opposing interests. This conflict of interests has manifested itself in several ways, not least of which is the lack of spirited opposition to marketisation from within its ranks. The presence of most, if not all, of the bureaucratic instruments on campus is the result of decisions favoured by UCU members who occupy management positions and who concur with the enforced "quality assurance" of higher education. Another problem is the dismal record of the union in committing funds or representing members to fight race discrimination cases, a fact possibly not unrelated to the union's own history of race relations.[55] Yet another problem – too great to consider in detail here – is the propensity for posturing in place of considered action. As one case in point, consider the following resolution, outlined by the union's Business for Equality Committee 2017,[56] "to work with the NUS and any other relevant group to highlight the impact cuts and fees have in trapping workers in the sex industry, and campaign for free access to education...(and) to support self-organised sex workers in their call for decriminalisation of sex work to allow collective working and improved safety for sex workers".

Fine words. Unfortunately, they take no heed of the NUS's own dismal record in supporting student sex workers or its own corporate takeover. It says nothing about what specific actions the union proposes to initiate. I must also regrettably note, for the record, the lack of any support that was forthcoming from the union when defending my own academic freedom to research student sex work. In this I was left to fend for myself. At the very least we need to be asking questions about why so many members view the union as a source of disappointment. It is not sufficient to dismiss these concerns by simply maintaining a blind faith just because it is the union.

If academics, managers and unions are so thoroughly ensnared in the maintenance of the neo-liberal order in universities, perhaps it is time to fundamentally rethink what the purpose of higher education is and what its role is in relation to the struggle to free our societies from regimes of domination and injustice. In this we must necessarily consider the tangled relationships between higher education, social class and the labour movement.

The distinguishing mark of all exile...is the refusal to be integrated – the determination to stand out from the physical space, to conjure up a place of one's own, different from the place in which those around are settled, a place unlike the places left behind and unlike the place of arrival
Zygmunt Bauman 2012, p.208

Chapter Five

The Re-invention of Education: Political Resistance and the Future

The political and economic forces fuelling crimes against humanity – whether they are unlawful wars, systematic torture, practiced indifference to chronic starvation, and disease or genocidal acts – are always mediated by educational forces
Giroux, cited in Hedges, 2009, p.92

Not one of us who has been trained to think critically and to write lucidly has the option to remain silent now
Parini, 2017

The prevailing myth of contemporary higher education is that its importance lies in the ability of its "consumers" to be successful – that is, to secure an esteemed, competitive, well-paid job in the dog eat dog economy of the disenchanted world. The esteemed jobs are those which are expected to throw a lifeline and ultimately cash to industries propping up the capitalist economy in its death throws.[57] This replaced an older myth promoting the impartial pursuit of knowledge and truth for the good of all. Alternative views of the value of education, beyond the noble and philanthropic or the contribution to the economy and the personal acquisition of money, fame and prestige, do exist but they are not heavily promoted within the realms of what has been termed the "military-industrial-academic" complex (Giroux, 2015). The bargain basement prizes in the halls of learning pertain to much rarer goods and serve other ends than bolstering the absence of morality in the technologies of misappropriation. To be believable, however, one must look further than the advertising hoardings, billboards and posters which adorn public space and proclaim the combined spectacle of knowledge, prosperity and leisure as the fruits of a university education.

The voices calling for a different life, meanwhile, are growing louder. The cultural myths of late capitalism, Boym tells us, no longer work; they are, in Bauman's view, no longer "suitable for the current *conditio humana*" (Bauman, 2012, vii). We are living in an epoch of civilisational upheaval. Everything is on the table, including an end to the interlocked corrupt order of injustice to which our esteemed educational establishments belong. It is time to reimagine not just learning, but the place of learning in the struggle for a just life for all. On the political stage, whether directed from the left or right, education has customarily been an object for reform – that is an object upon which political acts are directed to bring about change; change in the structure of the institutions of learning, the purposes which these serve for the economy and the *modus operandi* by which students and teachers are disciplined to accept the dominant ideological and utilitarian ethos. This ethos proclaims competition as an essential feature of life; reduces education to a system of rewards and punishments; demands attainments are measurable and quantifiable; that there are clear divisions between disciplines (even greater ones between intellectual and manual labour, the arts and sciences); that class relations are fixed in nature and in perpetuity and that to turn a profit is the supreme attainment in life. It gives rise to a world where, to quote the tag line of *L.A. Confidential*, "Everything is suspect...Everyone is for sale... and nothing is what it seems." Education under this imprimatur has never followed Walter Benjamin's (1999, p.147) exhortations to "discover the conditions of life" and to be "astonished at the circumstances". Instead it demands that we lie down in stupefied obedience, unconscious of the everyday marvels of existence, resigned to "accept the conditions of life" – which means to get on with it, lost in irrelevant scholarship and passive in relation to injustice. Outside of this institutional containment of learning and passion, contrasting images of the "the self-educated person" and "the university of life" drift in and out of the fog, sometimes presented as a reactionary antithesis to a formal education, sometimes not.

Marx caught sight of something beyond the stultifying horizons of imposed specialisation in his vision of the future worker, wiling away the hours, leap frogging from hunting to fishing, to cattle raising, to criticism. Marx's imaginative flight pertains to the desire to escape an intransigent economic system in which time has been reduced to clockwork, the boundaries between different forms of labour resemble prison walls and the opportunities to freely participate in all manner of social, "occupational", recreational and intellectual activities are restricted to the few. Freedom in Marx's view was to do with the possibilities which were revealed when alienation withered away. In the ongoing conditions of dystopia, freedom is a perpetual absence, a distance removed from the eternal improbable freedoms which exist in any given moment, even under conditions of domination.[58] Our concerns lie with the latter and the intellectual stances and positions that reside in the oft ignored decisional spaces of past, present and future time. The matter of what choices are available for academics and intellectuals to adopt in their working lives is necessarily inseparable from the kinds of intellectuals they are – by which I mean not the specific areas of scholarly interest within which an individual's labour unfolds but how she or he engages with them from a political standpoint.

Chomsky (1967, 2017), in his essays on the responsibility of intellectuals, distinguished between the obedient and the dissident, noting that the onus on both to "expose the lies of governments, to analyse actions according to their causes and motives and often hidden intentions" (Chomsky, 1967) was taken up rarely and only by the latter. The former, a majority, dutifully committed to following the path of least resistance, enact a "conformist, subservience to those in power" (Chomsky, 2004, p.48). Edward Said (1996) makes a similar distinction – between conformists and dissidents, marking the former as those who have no wish to disturb the status quo, the latter as passionately engaged in disturbing it, mindful of their public role in society to articulate a message from beyond the bounds of welcome opinion. Said, striking at the carefully cultivated image of lone intellectual endeavour, divorced from worldly concerns, maintains that it is precisely because of these contrasting attitudinal relations to power (whether of intellectuals or the intellectual community as a whole) that there can be no such thing as the private intellectual – indeed it is an oxymoron. Neoliberalism then has not just restructured the university; it has redefined the purpose of academic work. This it has done through strengthening and deepening the rewards for acquiescence to the status quo; the proliferation of previously esteemed academic titles to managers and bureaucrats; the grading of institutions and individuals (supposedly on the basis of academic merit but more realistically on the basis of class privilege and conformity), the distribution of academic prizes and the drive to specialisation combined with the elevation of some disciplines above others in terms of their potential for economic exploitation. Thus is the modern-day academic engineered, not to pursue the means to advance human freedom, knowledge or justice but to advance market freedom, market relevant knowledge and continued injustice. The abandonment of the grand narratives of emancipation and enlightenment owe less than is commonly thought to the strictures of post-modernist epistemology. That these lofty goals have fallen by the wayside is as much a result of the inherent pressure of the market to ignore them. The quest for universal values, rights and standards has been pushed aside in favour of the universal right of corporations to market access wherever they want it. As class resistance has receded before the onward march of the market, it has been replaced by an upsurge of sectional, though no less global, forms of struggle.

No doubt most, if not all, academics would take issue with an avowal that they wish to preserve the status quo. They are tasked, they would argue, with an unending search for new knowledge. But when Said refers to the status quo, it is not a stasis in the production of knowledge that he has in mind. It is the status quo writ large and small which surrounds the institutions of knowledge – the "fossilised", routinised nature of knowledge produced and the comfortable relations which exist between the forms, content and scope of knowledge and the current systems of power, privilege and oppression. All knowledge is inherently political – if for no other reason than it always speaks to its conditions of production. The task of the intellectual is to reveal and critique knowledge about the world, to interrogate our role in making it and to resist attempts, whether from individuals, institutions, corporations, governments or ideologies, to conceal undesirable truths. To "unearth the forgotten, to make connections that were denied" (Said, 1996, p.22) is the life blood of independent scholarship and an imperative for its survival. Investigation of the history (the social and collective memory) of academic disciplines, as they are understood, represented or misrepresented, is of pressing importance, because the attempts to rewrite the past (as well as the present) by those who possess the means to do so have never been greater. Who rewrites the past writes the future! A precondition for the neo-liberal collaboration with academia to endure is that the actual past has to be dismembered (dis-remembered), buried and ignored.

The burial is often a subtle one. In the topsy-turvy world of the twenty-first century the internment is often in the hands of those who manifest apparently liberal credentials and give the appearance of producing intellectual output. Consider, for example, the following; between April and September 2017, *The Guardian* newspaper ran 13 articles on mental health, many of them on the topic of anti-depressants. Six of these were opinion pieces, most were uncritical and rehearsed previously challenged views on the efficacy and mode of action of psychiatric drugs. One from Mark Brown (2017) stated that a recent "mega-analysis" (by Hieronymus et al., 2017) had answered "once and for all" the question of whether anti-depressants work. Brown, who has zero competence to assess research design or interpret scientific data, didn't let this stop him from declaring that depression was an "illness" and that the truth of anti-depressant efficacy was now established; that the study had found, "There was a clinically significant positive difference in people's mood when they were given the SSRI rather than a placebo."[59] In fact, the study Brown was referring to made no such claim about clinical significance and is in addition open to serious methodological objections. These include a failure to adequately control for the extent of side effects from anti-depressant use, or for expectancy effects arising from de-blinding (that is, when a participant in a trial correctly guesses whether they are receiving an active drug or a placebo it leads to expectations as to whether they will improve or not during the course of the trial) and the fact that the magnitude of the differences observed were so small as to have *no* clinical significance. In many instances comments from readers were invited below the articles. My own submission to one of these spaces in which I discussed the paucity of evidence for the efficacy of anti-depressants beyond a placebo effect (see Moncrieff, 2008; Kirsch, 2009) was removed. On questioning this the newspaper's moderator replied that:

in discussions regarding mental health we do not allow users to claim that issues such as depression do not exist. We consider this line of discussion dismissive and effectively off topic as per point 8 of our community standards – **Keep it relevant.** We know that some conversations can be wide-ranging, but if you post something which is unrelated to the original topic ("off-topic") then it may be removed, in order to keep the thread on track.

Further attempts to elicit a response, in which I pointed out that at no point had I stated that people are not depressed – an absurd claim – yielded no reply from the moderator and a reply from the newspaper's editor that the moderators had their full backing. Critical comment, informed by scientific evidence, it seems is "off-topic". All manner of unsubstantiated opinion is deemed "on track"! It appears that discussing the efficacy of this class of drugs is not permissible in articles about them. Presumably the readers are just there to absorb the conditioning and go on their merry, at times medicated, way. The paper's decision to effectively censor reader comment must be considered in relation to its financing. In 2002, it received $5 million from the Gates Foundation to promote both health and development issues. In the same year, the Gates Foundation bought shares in Big Pharma to the value of $205 million. *The Guardian* has clearly understood its backer's wishes – although its readers have no inkling of the tawdry connection which lies behind the attempt to govern what is permissible for them to think. To discuss the issue of funding and how it relates to content, however, is also forbidden, as is anything which contemplates, suggests or implies *The Guardian* may be biased – a hypothesis which they say is "against our community standards".

A BBC *Horizon* documentary (*Can we make a star on Earth?*) on the quest to produce power by nuclear fusion, which first aired in 2009 and again in 2017, provides a further telling example of how audiences are "educated" into the decontextualised corporate view of science as well as how conformist intellectuals are rewarded. In this programme, we are led on a global tour of Big Science fusion research by one-time pop star, media doyen and professor of particle physics Brian Cox. Among the jamboree of cutting edge physics, we are privy to a South Korean project which seeks to develop fusion energy by using high-energy lasers to compress a prospective fuel target – a process known as ICF (Internal Confinement Fusion). All very interesting but any discussion of its relation to nuclear weapons research is entirely missing from the gee-wiz spectacle. Fusion reactors have the potential to be used for military purposes (Franceschini, Englert and Liebert, 2013). The public presentation – and mystification – of science customarily strips away the political and commercial contexts in which the work unfolds. Without appropriate context, the public cannot appreciate the political significance of the science and its continued funding nor its contribution to the maintenance of global nuclear terror. There is a noble history of members of the physics community questioning the political uses to which its knowledge has been put – what Bronowski called "trying to buy the corpse of science".[60]

The BBC and Cox seem reluctant to appreciate just what these concerns are. For a physicist who is a champion of rational argument and no stranger to political comment, this reluctance to broach the wider political context of science – including the marketisation of the university – strips time itself out of the picture, as if everything on the screen bathes in the eternal waters of an unalterable truth. The enormity of what confronts us in the present day thus gives way to a rosy, uncomplicated view of alleged scientific benefits. Like the audience to Russell Crowe's cinematic gladiatorial exploits we are there only to be suitably "entertained" – observers of the grand spectacle of Big Science. Cox may be sympathetically viewed as a prisoner of his own success – a celebrity academic/scientist trapped within a BBC-engineered force field, aware that any critical comments about the toxic institutions of knowledge he represents, and their troubled relationship to capitalism, would mean arrivederci to the alluring prize of basking in the public eye, speaking about something he loves. More's the pity, because Cox is one of the few working-class voices in the media who speaks with any authority.

Finally, consider an example from The Independent, another icon of supposed left-wing journalism and like The Guardian a regular host to articles from journalist and quasi-fascist Julie Bindel, an advocate of the Nordic model of criminalising clients of sex workers and the view that all sex work is coercive and a form of violence against women. Bindel dismisses the views of sex workers who do not agree with her and shows a disdain for public debate. In work which she has published, her methods, research ethics and misrepresentation of existing scholarly literature have been unequivocally condemned by prominent researchers in the field. In a response to the "Big Brothel" project, which Bindel led, a list of prominent academics (See Sanders et al., 2008) noted of the work[61]:

> No reference is made to the fact that looking at research in the UK in the round shows a diversity of routes into prostitution, a diverse range of experiences within sex work and feelings about involvement. Sadly, the uni-directional focus upon sexual exploitation, sex as violence, vulnerability and social exclusion (all of which are real), the questionable means by which the Big Brothel 'research' was undertaken and the lack of engagement with the wider body of research, including Home Office studies, opens the study to criticisms, misrepresentations and bias.

Bindel's riposte was to state that the research undertaken wasn't from an academic institution and was important because of the media attention it attracted – criteria which have no bearing on the need for truth and integrity in research. Bindel's attitude to research ethics, as well as the accuracy of her presentation are consequently considered to be a serious problem by the wider academic community.

These examples show that sections of the mainstream

media often characterised as left leaning are quite content to produce material which is seriously misleading and allied to elite interests. The manner of delivery leads the public to expect that they are getting quality intellectual output when in fact it is devoid of the critical features one would normally expect to find in genuine intellectual content. In the media's manufacture of scientific investigation, the unpleasant truths (often commercial interest and power) behind the spectacle are not for consumption. Much of what masquerades as serious discussion of research in the media is little more than clickbait – a spectacle to seize the attention of passing readers and expose them to the accompanying advertising. What is in operation here is not just Bunuel's "phantom of liberty" but an even more surreal incarnation: "the fantasy of liberalism"!

Unfortunately, the media's shyness of the political context of research is mirrored by a good deal of university teaching. Shielding unpleasant truths and problematic histories is, in my experience, an intrinsic part of the way disciplinary knowledge is transmitted to students – little wonder that so many practitioners appear oblivious to the history of their own subjects or that so little pressure is generated from within to question the nefarious uses of scientific knowledge. Honesty in the face of this shady background ought to be something one could expect from the institutional hosts and supporters of research. Universities, supposedly the institutional guardians of the search for truth, are too often found in the role of guardians of the search for money.

The university as an institutional purveyor of knowledge exists in relation to wider systems of power as well as to the numerous individuals and groups who find a home within it to pursue knowledge. Discussion in this book of the neo-liberal takeover of higher education makes it clear that universities have forsworn any commitment to honesty, honour or truth in favour of "profit, control and efficiency" (Giroux, 2002, p.434).

Under current arrangements dissident intellectuals enjoy no support and cannot expect any to be forthcoming. Because of this, in the sense that Chomsky and Said envisage them, they remain isolated and marginalised figures; a sideshow, yet simultaneously the main attraction in any theatre of rebellious doubt. Critical thought always begins life on the margins – that is after all where the most interesting and unrestricted views are to be found, where the "tendencies at full swing in the 'centre' are, as a rule, most promptly spotted and most clearly articulated" (Bauman, 2012, p.141). "Exile", in Said's view, is the "model for the intellectual" (p.63). "The exilic intellectual", he writes, "does not respond to the logic of the conventional but to the audacity of the daring" (p.64). This entails experiments that can and are permitted to end in failure, ideas that may lead to dead ends, conventions to be upended, the acceptable to be unacceptable and vice versa, that risks the appropriation of its tools, methods and products in the fires of political reality.

But what of the relationship of intellectuals and the university to political struggle? There is an urgent need to rethink the place (and places) of learning, the role (and the nature) of intellectual activity and its value in the class-poisoned systems we inhabit. If the university cannot facilitate the freedom to challenge and resist established systems of power, is there any reason to suppose that political parties could fare any better? If the place of intellectual activity is to perennially question the world, to interrogate its history and introduce us to new perspectives, there is no reason to suppose that an organised political party of any persuasion will value such questioning of its own policies, platforms and processes for long. Loyalty and subservience to authority have always had a more fundamental role in party organisation and planning than intellectual enquiry. But can the two ever be reconciled? This is not to deny that the accommodation of intellectuals as fellow travellers, at least for a while, is possible while common goals are pursued. There is certainly much in the social science and medical literature to nourish and inform the plans of progressive political parties. But as Bauman has stated, there is an uncomfortable paradox at the heart of such an alliance, one which revolves around the relationship between individual ideas and collective practices. The more the latter are based on the former, the less are the former recognisable or defensible. Challenging ideas may easily mutate into unquestioned orthodoxy and yet the aspirations of critical thought are to reach out into the world and shape it. The ease with which rebellious thought is tamed, tailored and reconstructed to form the axiomatic base for questionable policy or future tyranny should not lead to a resigned acceptance of the futility of critical thought – rather it is just this history which necessitates that the critical option is pursued, in full recognition that loyalty can be tied only to that impulse and not to a given species of thought – undaunted by the weight of renowned personalities or portentous institutions.

If the purpose of higher education is to nurture and cultivate the capacity for independent thought, a criticality directed to historically-fashioned contemporary knowledge and the conditions of life which give rise to it, paradoxically the university may no longer be the best place in which to find it. How then can it be nourished outside the once gleaming ivory towers? Might other social institutions or forms of social organisation, yet unborn, be its future protectors? Even as efforts are made to resurrect the university or protect freedom of thought within its confines we must remember that there is nothing sacrosanct about it. It is an institution which was born of the Middle Ages, that rose in the midst and aftermath of the dark ages and which despite its clerical origins has no divine right to exist. The name university derives from the Latin *universitas magistrorum et scholarium*, a rough translation of which is a "community of teachers and scholars" (no mention there for administrators). As an institutional form, it has undergone continuous change – only in the early nineteenth century, at the University of Berlin, did it become a place where teaching and research go hand in hand in the search for truth. Nothing therefore guarantees its survival into the future. Anderson (2010) sees the "idea of the university" not as a fixed set of characteristics but as an institutional form dynamically seeking to resolve the tensions between teaching and research, autonomy and accountability and the respective roles to be taken in national and international culture. Freedom of thought has thus never been an absolute uncontaminated practice – rather an ideal to be defended, ever fragile and in need of support. He sees three possible developments – consolidation of a resource-intensive unitary mass higher education system; a more pluralistic system, where different universities seek to fulfil different missions and lastly acceptance of the death of the university and its takeover by utilitarian and managerial interests. All these possibilities, however, he envisages as unfolding under mainstream jurisdiction.

If on the contrary we accept as a working proposition the idea that intellectual thought can survive and flourish independent of mainstream institutional control then we can more readily appreciate Illich's (2002) contention that society needs to be "deschooled". In his eyes, formal education inculcates a disregard for one's own growth – an acceptance that other people should organise, direct and control what is learnt – a stance where "unmeasured experience" (p.40) slips through one's hands in the course of a collective journey to "spiritual suicide" (Illich, 2002, p.60). Successfully deschooling oneself accords with Gramsci's contention that anybody can be an intellectual. Gramsci's distinction between traditional and organic intellectuals is useful if we are to extend the non-capitalist function and purpose of the "university" beyond the campus and onto the streets and reconnect with the historical project of a system of teaching and learning free from state, church or corporate control. Gramsci's organic intellectual emerges from the community in which they reside, applying critical thought to the problems on hand. The Parisian protestors of 1968 dreamt of the "beach beneath the street", but perhaps more apt would be to realise, on the street, the library of human knowledge.

History has given us several telling instances of the emergence of "organic intellectuals", perhaps the most famous of which is Robben Island, where the leading opponents of the apartheid system were held prisoner. The "harshest, most iron-fisted outpost in the South African penal system" (Mandela, 1994, p.372) became known in the liberation movement as "the University". Mandela (1994, p.454) describes how "we became our own faculty, with our own professors, our own curriculum, our own courses". Employing a Socratic style of teaching, the courses taught included a systematic examination of the Black liberation struggle in South Africa as well as liberation struggles elsewhere. Mandela himself taught political economy. As he remarks, "We learned from each other." "History", Mandela wrote, "was at the heart of all our education," (above citation). This is a model of the university as a spontaneous creation which arises to meet the needs of a time and place.

The "Anti-University of London" was an experimental project in communal living and self-organised education set up in Shoreditch (Rivington Street), East London in February 1968, following the Dialectics of Liberation conference of the preceding year.[62] Promoting an ideology of counter culture knowledge and free expression, the Anti-University, as Alan Krebs, one of the founders commented, shunned the notion of "education as a licence to practice in the establishment", a far cry from the university as factory (Alibhai-Brown, 2013) we see today. The courses on offer covered a variety of aspects of contemporary arts, politics and existential psychiatry, including specific offerings on Black Power, The Future of Capitalism, Counter Culture and Revolution. R.D. Laing, David Cooper, Francis Huxley, Joe Berke, Jeff Nuttall, Juliet Mitchell, Stokely

Carmichael and Yoko Ono were among the luminaries who gave lectures there. The project lasted a year before the premises were reclaimed by landlords, though one of its longer lasting legacies was the renowned Compendium Bookshop. Another is the collaborative experiment "Anti-University Now", (http://www. antiuniversity.org/) begun in 2015, which each summer runs a week-long festival and develops programmes throughout the year, the stated aims of which are "to challenge institutionalised education, access to learning and the mechanism of knowledge creation and distribution", offering an "open invitation to teach and learn *any subject, in any form, anywhere*".

The University at Robben Island and the Anti-Universities of yesteryear and today belong to the "dissenting histories of our present" (Boym, 2017, p.32); off-modern excursions in pursuit of the licence to practice rebellion, that most obscure and precious object of intellectual desire. As trial runs at a new institutional and community order, they reveal a willingness to redraw the parameters within which we think the rules of the educational game are played and employ a pedagogical strategy which contends with the societal play of forces beneath the surface conventions of academic discourse and the knowledge economy. A world away from the aesthetic aloof enclave exemplified in Hesse's *The Glass Bead Game* or the construction of education as an industry, they pose questions about the nature, function and purpose of information in an oppressive society and the relation between scholarship and wisdom. They also challenge taken for granted notions of the distinction – a hierarchical one at that – between the givers and receivers of knowledge. Were the transmission, generation and construction of knowledge reconsidered as acts of co-creation and not individual ones, we might be better placed to view education as a primarily social or group activity, at odds with the grading and sorting of individuals. Teaching, properly done, becomes a learning activity for everyone involved. Delivering a "lecture", I have always thought, presents an opportunity for thinking through issues. It is a more effective and reflective process when there is a genuine conversation, a dialogue underway with students, one which is mindful of the "tapestry of lived life" (Benjamin, 1999, p.198) outside the lecture hall and where nobody is on trial. Even when there is fundamental disagreement, one can more quickly grasp the structural nature – the topography of the discord – and with enough attention over sufficient time, discern the direction of necessary travel in the search for resolution.

The ways and means by which understanding arrives, and precisely when, is never entirely predictable. Clarity can emerge in an instant and yet also require years of devotion, both contemplative and practical. The best university education may be of this type – where space and time is set aside for deep problems, which may exceed current capacities for assimilation or solution and which require a tolerance for uncertainty and ambiguity, that is, a suspension of belief in the necessity for the world to make sense. The modalities and structures binding the timetables of official learning – the 50-minute lesson/lecture, courses, terms, semesters, modules, degrees – pre-packaged bite size "products" for the market, are all artificial, built around the convenience of an educational "store" which makes patient self-directed learning more difficult. These temporal rituals enable the state to not only appropriate and define education, but under the cover of darkness to sneak dependency and passivity into the unconscious construction of the classroom drama. Slowing down, far from being an inevitable precursor to being left behind, may be the best means we all have (both on and beyond the campus) for taking stock, looking (and planning) ahead and avoiding the undesirable attractions of a prefabricated political nostalgia.

It is important, in the quest to defend the diminishing public educational and intellectual spaces, that the practices which they embody – and indeed the insights which they produce – are translated into political resources for activists, and taken up as tools for the creation of inroads into official thinking. The learning and sharing of skills and knowledge must branch out from its current institutional restrictions and see the skills and knowledge become networked community resources, comprising people, tools and appropriate spaces. The "university", the community of scholars in the virtual age, requires no fixed physical substratum, no domineering architecture of official power towering over the landscape of possible thought. It is an idea, alluding to a cosmopolitan web of human relationships, both real and virtual, spanning past, present and future, committed to the necessary freedoms and actions which independent thought is predicated upon and from which one may draw sustenance, simply by knowing others are out there similarly engaged.

Away from the question of institutional political relationships there is another pressing problem, which in the UK, if not the US, haunts the possibility of the intellectual development of the left. There are several interlocking aspects to this, the first of which relates to the marked increases in social mobility in the post war period – a change which for the first time opened up higher education to people from working-class backgrounds. Ryan and Sackrey (1984) detail the personal costs confronting those newly-arrived strangers to the academy. Their arrival saw them regarded as outsiders by the traditional incumbents and cast to the margins by those in their home areas. Social mobility into the academy entailed cultural migration from one home, often happy to wave the emigres goodbye, to another less than welcoming one. The ambiguous relationship between the working class and higher education and the separation of intellectual thought from organised labour in many ways begins here – though it is also true that the Cartesian distinction between the work of the mind and that of the body is centuries old. The art critic John Berger (2016, xv) wrote that to migrate "is always to dismantle the centre of the world, and so move to a lost disoriented one". The migration of the working class has opened up a view of the nature of the social world to which we have yet to acclimatise. Old privileges in the ordering of the world stubbornly persist. It is not just the migrants who remain disoriented by class; collectively we remain all at sea, at the mercy of the centuries-old tides of capitalism, class, forgotten memory and the winds blowing from the past shipwrecks of humanity. But to know, at the very least, that we are lost and far from home is a step in the right direction for the reclamation of hope.

Second, despite the sweeping social changes, higher education retains its status as a luxury and because of this it constitutes a continuing source of pain for those on the other side of the fence who have not accessed it. Prior to the mass expansion of higher education in the 1990s this pain was more widely distributed and was in some sense more visible and commonly understood by the majority who never became students. Mass enrolment, however, has exposed in its wake a smaller group of disgruntled, dissatisfied "non-consumers" of education. These comprise not just the less able or the more traumatised sections of society whose learning opportunities have been impeded by misfortune but a group who, from within their own locality, over generations have mapped out a culturally supported absence of desire or belief in education; who have never viewed it as a vehicle to transcend economic deprivation and who are, as a group, antagonistic towards its fruits. They have become prey to the xenophobic nostalgia for an illusory past only because they have already abandoned a place in the future. In one sense, they have laid claim to a distinct psycho-geographical territory – in a feared and forgotten undergrowth of class relations, a place neglected for so long that its loss from our collective understanding of the injuries of class means we can discern its origins only with great effort and difficulty. I do not say this to imply education is a global panacea to inequality, for it is not, but that its active exclusion from the field of possible horizons for one section of the working-class signals something deeply troubling.

Third, the distance between the intellectual centre of the Labour movement – which has grown to endorse feminism, anti-racism, multiculturalism and disability politics – and many of those left ravaged by austerity politics has grown into a chasm. The overlap between the less advantaged from these processes – the majority of whom are white, English, urban and working class – has stirred up a political hornet's nest in a further aftershock to the 2008 financial crisis. Alienation from education and intellectual thought and alienation from the economy have combined to create a sizeable number of people who are disaffected with progressive politics, susceptible to anti-immigration rhetoric and distrustful of "experts", whose opinions they treat with suspicion. Messages targeted to these groups comprised a central feature of the Leave side in the EU referendum campaign. At the same time, the official aversion to expert opinion is manifest in increasingly diverse ways. Corporate actors, for example, loyal to the fossil fuel industry, are willing to spend vast sums of money to deny climate change, fearing that authoritative opinion is turning against them. Then there is the UK government, hell-bent on the privatisation of health services, instructing the medical profession as to how it ought to interpret data on weekend mortality rates. Once again, however, the media presents the divergence as intellectually credible in the face of almost no credible intellectual opinion supporting it. While both corporate and government interpretations of scientific data tend to find few friends within the scientific community, there is, in addition to these official variants of misinformation, the corrosive effect of money in mainstream research, notably evident in the intertwining of biological psychiatry and Big Pharma. This makes for a toxic and perplexing brew – one which will do nothing to allay public uncertainty as to what in the public domain can and cannot be trusted.

The problem resulting from this tapestry of class despair, anger and bewilderment is not just the immediate one of how to reach disaffected groups (whose aversion to rational argument and support for nationalist and racist policies is dragging the country over a political and economic cliff with fascism waiting at the bottom) but how to heal the educational breach which has been running through the labour movement and the working class for decades. This is an issue which is virtually taboo and although its effects dominate the political landscape, it functions as the socio-economic equivalent of dark matter. Members of the working class in many migrant groups have continued to regard education as a resource, which objectively enhances life chances and existentially functions as a means of individual and collective salvation; so, the question as to why a specific group of English people have not must be understood.

Claims that the education system fails white working-class boys (but not girls) (for example, Rhodes, 2016) badly miss the point. Of course, it is relevant that working class identity – a male working-class identity at that – built on the seeds of industrialisation has been starkly undermined by years of deindustrialisation, but there is nothing intrinsic to that reality that should provoke a scornful attitude to education. No one appears willing to say that, just as forms of masculinity may be toxic, which it is recognised men themselves must address, where working-class cultures have adopted toxic norms they cannot be excused or exonerated from the burden of responsibility for doing something about it. Accepting denial of responsibility in an age where selfish endeavour is endorsed by neo-liberal doctrine cannot lead to any happy end. To deny agency is to compound the historically embedded injustices, injuries and indignities. Bad choices have been made and it is hard not to see the decision to abandon hope in a life-changing resource as a form of acquiescence to class rule which has been progressively concentrated through generations of families, leaving behind fossilised structures of thought and feeling. Laing and colleagues opened up for consideration the proposition that the recurrence of mental health issues in successive generations owed little to genetics and a good deal more to dysfunctional behaviours and patterns of communication which were repeated, learnt through experience and passed on to offspring. This is behaviour as a form of social memory. We need to extend this "archaeological" analysis of social relations beyond the family, to communities and places where forms of internalised oppression, subjugation, violence and political reaction have become entrenched; congealed forms of historical process living in the thoughts and practices of people today.

Sennet and Cobb (1973, p.258) remarked, not without irony, that it was "the way in which people try to keep free of the emotional grip of the social structure" that "unintentionally, systematically, in aggregate keeps the class order going". The ubiquitous narrative of victimhood, paralysing and growing daily, must be paused for us to take stock of this irony. We are all wretched, colonised subjects in the imperium of capital and have found our way here to some degree under our own steam. To pause and rethink our own role in the world may be crucial to ongoing efforts to supplant the horror story of neo-liberalism with a new tale. It is not made easy by the increasing state and corporate control of higher education, which, without prior warning, teaches subordination as an economic good and goes out of its way to divorce the practice of intellectual labour from the struggle for social justice. It is not putting too fine a point on it to say that with education, both formal and informal, the future is at stake. In the UK, one in seven of all undergraduates and one in five postgraduates now study business and management – in over 100 business schools. This signals a takeover of higher learning of truly alarming proportions, a surreptitious eradication of so many tomorrows in an insatiable homily to money. In *The Future of Nostalgia,* Svetlana Boym (2001, xiii) described the toxic ruins of the Russian city of Kaliningrad – once Prussian Konigsberg – as resembling a "theme park of lost illusions". In the necessity to prise the golden apple of education back from the fevered hands of the market, we must do everything possible to rescue it from a similar fate.

Endnotes

1. Halsey and O'Brien (2014).
2. Roberts (2010).
3. Streeck (2016).
4. See Dyhouse (2007); Blake (2010) for a fuller timeline and discussion of funding changes.
5. See "The Castle" in *The Essential Kafka* (2014, p.276).
6. In contrast to journal impact factors, a range of author impact metrics also exist. The most well-known of these is the h-index, defined as the number of papers written by a scholar which have been cited in other papers at least h times. For example, h=15 when an author has 15 publications, each of which has been cited at least 15 times. The attraction of metrics to some people has a lot to do with the pseudo-legitimacy conferred by anything remotely mathematical.
7. In fact, in the Australian equivalent – the Excellence in Research for Australia – results are summarised by rating research performance on a scale of 1–5, where a score of 5 indicates "performance well above world standard". See Izak, Kostera and Zawadzki (2017).
8. Lucrative for the state and the corporate sector as UK students pay eye-watering fees – in effect subsidising the costs of their own training.
9. I stress, from my perspective. The manager in question may believe in the utmost sincerity of what comes across as utterly insincere. A psychoanalytic examination of the possible alienation and auto-mystification of one's own experience that may be going on here is beyond the scope of the present discussion. It may, however, be a pre-requisite for modern university management.
10. Possibly an apt truncation of Kafkaesque economics.

11. Italy – from Dante's La Divina Commedia, Canto XXXIII, line 80.

12. Even stalwarts of the profession such as Jerome Kagan (2012) have begun to question just exactly what has come out of it.

13. Research suggests higher social class is associated with more unethical behaviour (Piff et al., 2012). See also https://network23.org/kingston/2017/09/26/corruption-in-the-smt/ for further allegations of financial impropriety. That *The Guardian* chose to have the person who is the subject of these allegations write about higher education finance shortly afterwards (see McQuillan, 2017) should be considered one of life's ironies.

14. See Peter Scott (2010) who, when Vice-Chancellor of Kingston University, described his VC colleagues as "active collaborators" offering only "feeble resistance" to the "deepest cuts ever in university funding and the threat of privatisation".

15. The excessive pay of vice-chancellors has led to them being described as resembling "a self-serving cartel" (see Khomami, 2017).

16. Here's an illustrative example of such nonsense currently on show at the theatre of the academic absurd; according to Nick Hillman, director of the Higher Education Policy Institute, as of June 2017, between 30 and 40 UK universities currently claim to be in the top 10 (Weale, 2017). And in another, the *Times Higher Education* in October 2014 combined the results of three league tables, including its own, despite a caveat which acknowledged the "methodological limitations" and absence of "statistical rigour" in the exercise. The irony of printing an admission of the worthless nature of what's just appeared was probably lost on the *THE*. See *THE*, 2173, p.11.

17. Apologies to Philip K. Dick.

18. I have since discovered an earlier reference, dating from 1995, of student nurses turning to prostitution because of the low levels of bursaries and grants (*Nursing Standard*, 1995).

19. One fifth of the sample were working 30 hours per week, some up to 50 hours.

20. I contributed a piece to *The Guardian* (Roberts, 1999) and was subsequently interviewed by the BBC for the main lunchtime news programme and for the BBC World Service (see also BBC News Online, 2001).

21. In a more recent longitudinal study, Richardson, Elliot, Roberts and Jansen (2017) confirmed that financial difficulties lead to poor mental health in students, with the possibility of a vicious cycle in play.

22. Others have described this "respectability" as the "gentrification of the sex industry" (see for example Grant, 2014, p.7).

23. At the time of writing, fees are £9,250 for England, £4,030 for Northern Ireland and £4,046 for Wales after grants are factored in; Scotland is omitted from the estimate as home students there pay no tuition fees.

24. A review of available evidence suggests female sex workers who have greater autonomy in their jobs enjoy better working conditions and have greater job satisfaction enjoy much better mental health than other groups of sex workers (see Sanders et al., 2017).

25. Also described as totalitarian capitalism – See Monbiot (2017).

26. A full list of the signatory institutions is given here http://www.magna-charta.org/signatory-universities

27. For example, Balfour and Allen's (2014) report on sex work and social exclusion is misrepresented (p.27) as describing student sex work as more likely to be a "lifestyle choice". Balfour and Allen can legitimately be criticised for arguing

that student sex workers do not face high levels of social exclusion, but they do not refer to their activities in the sex industry as a lifestyle choice.

28. These market influences, Hedgecoe suggests, produce a set of practices which include hierarchical work relations, audit and league tables, a drive towards corporate funded research and a strategy of reputation management.

29. The ESRC is one of the seven funding councils in the UK.

30. As a footnote on reputational protection, a student journalist let me know that several managers from the university to which he belonged had sought to trash my reputation and convince him that the research on students' roles in sex work had no merit. An interesting insight into the organisational ethics pursued in some institutions of learning and the one-sided nature of reputation management.

31. I betray my Catholic origins – but in the universities' quest to aspire to the sacred in knowledge one can't help but feel that they have settled for the profane.

32. See *Psychology and Capitalism* (Roberts, 2015) for more on this.

33. See Laura Agustin (2007) for an examination of the lived experiences of migrant workers who sell sexual services and a critique of the "rescue industry". One of her conclusions is that we would do well to abandon the myth of a clear boundary between commercial sex and many normalised sexual activities.

34. All prime techniques of power. See Bauman (2012).

35. The Education Reform Act 1988 is available at http://www.legislation.gov.uk/ukpga/1988/40/contents

36. The EAT is responsible for handling appeals against decisions made by an employment tribunal where a legal mistake may have been made in the case.

37. See http://www.bailii.org/ew/cases/EWHC/QB/2013/196.html for the judgment in this case.

38. Gillies and Edwards (2017, p.96) define psychological governance as "attempts to advance, manage and regulate the social good through targeting the minds of individuals as a means of changing their behaviour".

39. See Furedi (2016).

40. A report by the Institute for Public Policy Research (Thorley, 2017) notes that in 2015 there were 134 suicides at UK universities. Most institutions do not routinely keep figures. Despite noting, however, that debt is a significant source of stress for students, the IPPR report contains no recommendations for addressing this. See also Jenkin (2017).

41. The French "Second Left" being one such exception.

42. One of the curious features of the triumph of identity politics on campus is that student identity has proven to be a weak base for political struggle despite the exploited position students occupy. That is, no strong collective identity as students has been reciprocally internalised and championed. As such it is an "identity" unlike others – politically significant and widespread yet peripheral and ephemeral.

43. A Foucauldian position on the history of scientific thought would have to, of necessity, de-emphasise the creative contributions of notable individuals, for example, Copernicus, Galileo, Newton, Darwin, Einstein and so on in favour of an account which *entirely* favoured the social, economic and historical conditions for knowledge. The subject, robbed of agency, then functions as a passive vessel through which the flowing structures of historical thought are experienced.

44. See the Chomsky-Foucault, 2006 debate, pp.138–139 for more on this.

45. A poisoned chalice one might say, drawing on the German connotations of the word for poison (gift).

46. Let the buyer beware. The situation is a classic example of information asymmetry in the market place in which defects in the good or service may be hidden from the buyer, and are known only to the seller.

47. We must not forget that students are badgered, some would say hounded, to complete the survey and that many will be offered various "inducements" to give higher scores. Calls by the NUS to boycott the survey have generally not been very successful – something possibly connected to the low esteem with which the union is regarded by students. The year 2017, however, marks an exception. The boycott, called in protest against the TEF, led to several major universities, including Oxford, Cambridge, Manchester and Sheffield, not being included in the tables.

48. In two thirds of UK universities, administrators now outnumber academics (THE, 2015). The idea that the administrative class needs to be "won over" for a reversal of neo-liberalism in academia to occur is misguided. Zebra on the African savannah might similarly hope for lions to develop a taste for vegetarianism.

49. These are considered predominantly female jobs. In contrast, jobs performed by males which necessitate body work, that is, work on the bodies of others – as in the protective and security services – are frequently under direct surveillance. See Wolkowitz et al. (2013) for further exploration of these issues.

50. Scambler presents six categories of sex worker; Coerced, Destined, Survivors, Workers, Opportunists and Bohemians. These reflect different motivations, needs and trajectories.

51. Entitled *How the 'Real World' at last became a Myth* (Nietzsche, 1968, p.40).

52. See Kim (2011) for a wider discussion of the neo-liberal transformation and governance of young femininity.

53. https://www.sussex.ac.uk/webteam/gateway/file.php?nam

e=westmarland-review.pdf&site=303

54. https://www.ucu.org.uk/policyhub

55. Something I can attest to from personal experience. See also https://sites.google.com/site/cemkumar/davidtriesman-joannadegroot%26racismonfloo

56. https://www.ucu.org.uk/article/8802/Business-of-the-Equality-Committee-2017#56

57. The so-called STEM subjects – science, technology, engineering and medicine – figure prominently among them.

58. See my discussion of the differences between alienation and estrangement in *The Off-Modern: Psychology Estranged* (Roberts, 2017).

59. Selective Serotonin Reuptake Inhibitor (SSRI) – one class of anti-depressants.

60. Cited in Ferris (1983, p.36).

61. I was one of the academics to put my name to the critique.

62. See http://antihistory.org/ and http://greatwen.com/2010/12/15/the-london-anti-university/ for a collection of articles, press cuttings, videos and texts.

References

Adams, P. (2017) "Poorest students will finish university with £57,000 debt, says IFS". *The Guardian*, 5 July. https://www.theguardian.com/education/2017/jul/05/poorest-students-will-finish-university-with-57000-debt-says-ifs   Accessed July 2017.

Alibhai -Brown, Y. (2013) "When did university become a factory?" *The Independent*, 18 August. http://www.independent.co.uk/voices/comment/when-did-university-become-a-factory-8773207.html?origin=internalSearch Accessed August 2013.

Anderson, R. (2010) "The 'Idea of a University' today. History and Policy", 1 March. http://www.historyandpolicy.org/policy-papers/papers/the-idea-of-a-university-today Accessed September 2017.

Appleton. J. (2016) *Officious. Rise of the busy body state*. Winchester. Zero Books.

Augustin, L.M. (2007) *Sex at the margins. Migration, labour markets and the rescue industry*. London. Zed Books.

Alldred, P. and Miller, T. (2007) "Measuring what's valued or valuing what's measured? Knowledge production and the Research Assessment Exercise". In V. Gillies and H. Lucey (eds) *Power, knowledge and the academy*. (pp.147–167). Houndmills. Palgrave.

Anonymous (2012) "Confessions of a student prostitute". *Student BMJ*, 20, e906.

Arendt, H. (1976) *The origins of totalitarianism*. London. Harvest.

Bachan, R. (2015) "Grade inflation in UK higher education". *Studies in Higher Education*, 42(8), 1580–1600.

Back, L. (2016) *Academic Diary*. London. Goldsmiths Press.

Bailey, M. (2015) "The strange death of the liberal university". *Open Democracy*. https://www.opendemocracy.net/michael-bailey/strange-death-of-liberal-university Accessed July 2017.

Bailey, M. and Freedman, D. (2011) *The assault on universities. A manifesto for resistance.* London. Pluto Press.

Balfour, R. and Allen, J. (2014) "A Review of the Literature on Sex Workers and Social Exclusion". UCL Institute of Health Equity for Inclusion Health, Department of Health. https://www.gov.uk/government/uploads/system/uploads/attachment_data/file/303927/A_Review_of_the_Literature_on_sex_workers_and_social_exclusion.pdf Accessed July 2017.

Barclays News Release (2000) "Graduate debt soars as Barclays launch new package to ease financial pressure", 18 April.

Barrett, D. (1997) "Students on the game", *The Times Higher Education Supplement,* 18 July.

Bauman, Z. (2012) *Liquid modernity.* London. Polity.

BBC News Online (2001) "Hard-up students 'turn to vice'". http://news.bbc.co.uk/1/hi/education/1303782.stm Accessed April 2001.

BBC News Online (2008) "University staff faking survey". http://news.bbc.co.uk/1/hi/education/7397979.stm Accessed June 2017.

BBC News Online (2010) "Students working in sex trade increases over 10 years". http://news.bbc.co.uk/1/hi/england/8568723.stm Accessed March 2010.

BBC News Online (2011a) "After scandal, what happens now to University of Wales?" http://www.bbc.co.uk/news/uk-wales-15463655 Accessed July 2017.

BBC News Online (2011b) "NUS: Students turning to prostitution to fund studies". http://www.bbc.co.uk/news/education-16157522 Accessed December 2011.

BBC News Online (2011c) "NUS criticised over tuition fees memo". http://www.bbc.co.uk/news/education-12492825 Accessed July 2017.

BBC News Online (2014) "Students could be paying loans

into their 50s – report". http://www.bbc.co.uk/news/education-26954901 Accessed January 2015.

BBC News Online (2016) "England degree debt 'highest in English-speaking world'". http://www.bbc.co.uk/news/education-36150276 Accessed April 2016.

Beaumont, M. (2015) *Night walking*. London. Verso.

Benjamin, W. (1999) *Illuminations*. London. Pimlico.

Berger, J. (2016) *Landscapes: John Berger on Art.* London. Verso.

Bernstein, E. (2007) "Sex work for the middle classes". *Sexualities* 10, (4), 473–488.

Betzer, F., Kohler, S. and Schlemm, L. (2015) "Sex Work Among Students of Higher Education: A Survey-Based, Cross-Sectional Study". *Archives of Sexual Behaviour*, 44, 525–528.

Bird, S.M., Cox, D., Farewell, V.T., Goldstein, H., Holt, T. and Smith, P.C. (2005) "Performance Indicators: Good, Bad, and Ugly". *Journal of the Royal Statistical Society, Series A (Statistics in Society)*, 168 (1), 1–27.

Blake, H. (2010) "Grants, loans and tuition fees: a timeline of how university funding has evolved". http://www.telegraph.co.uk/education/educationnews/8057871/Grants-loans-and-tuition-fees-a-timeline-of-how-university-funding-has-evolved.html Accessed August 2012.

Boym, S. (1994) *Common Places. Mythologies of everyday life in Russia*. Cambridge. Harvard University Press.

Boym, S. (2001) *The future of nostalgia*. New York. Basic Books.

Boym, S. (2017) *The Off-Modern*. London. Bloomsbury.

Braben, (2008) "RAE reaction: Shoot for the blue skies". *Times Higher Education Supplement*, 22 December. http://www.timeshighereducation.co.uk/story.asp?storycode=404793 Accessed March 2009.

Brinkworth, L. (2007) "Students who sell sex". *Cosmopolitan*, July, 60–62.

Brown, J. (2013) "Institutions 'bury heads in sand' over students' sex work". http://www.independent.co.uk/student/news/

sex-for-tuition-fees-are-universities-just-refusing-to-face-up-to-the-facts-8667648.html Accessed June 2013.

Brown, M. (2017) "Antidepressants work, so why do we shame people for taking them?" *The Guardian*, 1 September. https://www.theguardian.com/commentisfree/2017/sep/01/antidepressants-work-shame-people-ssri Accessed September 2017.

Brown, R. (2006) "Never mind the feel". *Academy Exchange*, 4, 12–13.

Buranyi, (2017) "Is the staggeringly profitable business of scientific publishing bad for science?" *The Guardian* https://www.theguardian.com/science/2017/jun/27/profitable-business-scientific-publishing-bad-for-science Accessed June 2017.

Burnes, T.R., Long, S.L. and Schept, R. A. (2012) "A resilience-based lens of sex work: Implications for professional psychologists". *Professional Psychology: Research and Practice*, 43(2), 137–144. doi: 10.1037/a0026205

Calvino, I. (1997) *Invisible Cities*. London. Vintage.

Channel 4 News (2012) "Hard-up students seek help from sugar daddy website". http://www.channel4.com/news/hard-up-students-seek-help-from-sugar-daddy-website Accessed May 2012.

Chapleo, C. (2011) "Branding a university: adding real value or 'smoke and mirrors'?" In M. Molesworth, R. Scullion and E. Nixon (eds) *The marketizing of higher education and the student as consumer* (pp.101–114). London. Routledge.

Chomsky, N. (1967). "The responsibility of intellectuals". *New York Review of Books*, 8(3). Supplement.

Chomsky, N. (2004). *Hegemony or Survival: America's quest for global dominance*. London: Penguin.

Chomsky, N. (2017) *Who rules the world?* London. Penguin.

Chomsky, N. and Foucault, M. (2006) *The Chomsky-Foucault debate on Human Nature*. London. The New Press.

Cockburn, H. (2017) "Number of first class university degrees soars amid grade inflation warning". *The Independent,* 20 July. http://www.independent.co.uk/News/education/education-university-grade-first-numbers-soar-grade-inflation-warning-a7849936.html Accessed July 2017.

Cocozza, P. (2017) "The party's over – how tuition fees ruined university life". *The Guardian,* 11 July. https://www.theguardian.com/education/2017/jul/11/the-partys-over-how-tuition-fees-ruined-university-life#comment-101908341 Accessed July 2017.

Cohen, S. (2001) *States of denial.* Cambridge. Polity.

Connelly, R., Sullivan, A. and Jerrim, J. (2014) "Primary and secondary education and poverty review". London. Centre for Longitudinal Studies. Institute of Education, August.

Confucius (2000). *The Analects.* London. Everyman Publishers.

Conrad, J. (2012) *Heart of darkness.* London. Penguin.

Cooper, D. (1971) *The death of the family.* London. Penguin.

Crawford, C. and Jin, W. (2012) "Payback time? Student debt and loan repayments: what will the 2012 reforms mean for graduates?" Institute of Fiscal Studies. IFS Report R93.

Debord, G. (1992) *The Society of the Spectacle.* New York. Zone Books.

Dixon, J. (2012) "Medical schools' attitudes towards student prostitution". *Student BMJ,* 20, 16–18.

Dolman, K. (2008) "Selling sex to study". https://www.thetimes.co.uk/article/selling-sex-to-study-dswswrrf56g Accessed February 2008.

Dyhouse, C. (2007) "Going to university: funding, costs, benefits". http://www.historyandpolicy.org/policy-papers/papers/going-to-university-funding-costs-benefits Accessed August 2012.

Eccleston, K. and Hayes, D. (2009) *The dangerous rise of therapeutic education: How teaching Is becoming therapy.* London. Routledge.

Eccleston, K. (2017) "Therapeutic governance of psycho-emotionally vulnerable citizens". In J. Pykett, R. Jones and

M. Whitehead (eds) *Psychological governance and public policy* (pp.56–74). London. Routledge.

Economic and Social Research Council (ESRC) (2010) *Framework for Research Ethics*. Swindon. ESRC.

Evans, M. (2004) *Killing thinking: The death of the university*. London. Continuum.

European Court of Human Rights (ECHR) (1998) European Convention of Human Rights. European Court of Human Rights Council of Europe F-67075 Strasbourg cedex. http://www.echr.coe.int/Documents/Convention_ENG.pdf Accessed June 2011.

European University Association (2007) *Lisbon declaration. Europe's Universities beyond 2010*. Brussels.

Farrington, D. and Palfreyman, D. (2012) *The Law of Higher Education* (2nd Edition), Oxford. Oxford University Press.

Faulkner, N. (2011) "What is a University Education for?" In M. Bailey and D. Freedman (eds) *The assault on universities. A manifesto for resistance* (pp.27–36). London. Pluto.

Ferris, T. (1983) "The other Einstein". *Science,* 4(3), 34–41.

Fisher, M. (2009) *Capitalist realism. Is there no alternative?* Winchester. Zero Books.

Fisher, M. (2017) "'It's not your fault': Consciousness-raising as a reversal of magical voluntarism". *Clinical Psychology Forum,* 297, 4–7.

Franceschini, G., Englert, M. and Liebert, W. (2013) "Nuclear Fusion Power for Weapons Purposes". *The Nonproliferation Review*, 20 (3), 525–544.

Fromm, E. (1976) *To have or to be?* London. Bloomsbury.

Furedi, F. (2011) "Introduction to the marketisation of higher education and the student as consumer". In M. Molesworth, R. Scullion and E. Nixon (eds) *The marketisation of teaching and learning in higher education* (pp.1–7). New York. Routledge.

Furedi, F. (2016) *What's happened to the university?* London. Routledge.

Galeano, E. (1998) *Upside Down. A primer for the looking glass world*. New York. Picador.

Gambetta, D., and Origgi, G. (2013). "The LL game the curious preference for low quality and its norms". *Politics, Philosophy and Economics*, 12(1), 3–23.

Gillies, V. F. And Edwards, R. (2017) "'What about the children?' Re-engineering citizens of the future". In J. Pykett, R. Jones and M. Whitehead (eds) *Psychological governance and public policy* (pp.96–115). London. Routledge.

Giroux, H. (2014) *Neoliberalism's War on Higher Education*. Haymarket Books. Chicago.

Giroux, H. (2015) *The University in Chains: Confronting the Military-Industrial-Academic Complex*. London. Routledge.

Girresch, A. (2011) "Students by day, strippers by night: Transactional sexuality among Indiana college students". *Journal of History and Social Science*, Fall.

Goldhill, O. and Bingham, J. (2015) "One in three UK female students sexually assaulted or abused on campus". *The Telegraph*, 14 January. http://www.telegraph.co.uk/women/womens-life/11343380/Sexually-assault-1-in-3-UK-female-students-victim-on-campus.html Accessed August 2017.

Goldstein, H. and Leckie, G. (2008) "School league tables: what can they really tell us?" *Significance*, June, 67–69.

Goodman, A., Sibieta, L. and Washbrook, E. (2009) "Inequalities in educational outcomes among children aged 3 to 16". Final report to the National Equality Panel. Centre of Market and Public Organisations. https://www.yumpu.com/en/document/view/32060965/inequalities-in-educational-outcomes-among-children-aged-3-home Accessed August 2017.

Grant, M.G. (2014) *Playing the whore*. London. Verso.

Greatorex, P. (2013a) "Telling tales out of school". *Local Government Lawyer*, 27 February http://www.localgovernmentlawyer.co.uk/index.php?option=com_content&view=article&id=134

10%3Atelling-tales-out-of-school&catid=49%3Acomment-a-analysis-articles&Itemid=9 Accessed March 2013.

Greatorex, P. (2013b) "Protecting the reputation of schools and universities". https://education11kbw.com/protecting-the-reputation-of-schools-and-universities/ Accessed March 2013.

Gutting, G. (2005) *Foucault. A very short introduction.* Oxford. Oxford University Press.

Halsey, J. and O'Brien, K. (2014) "Education markets in English and American universities". In Pickard, S (2015) *Higher Education in the UK and the US: Converging University Models in a Global Academic World.* Leiden. Brill Academic Publishing. pp.35–58.

Hansard (1999) "Student Debt". House of Lords, 4 March, Column 1791–1793.

Hartley, D. (1995) "The 'McDonaldization' of Higher Education: food for thought?" *Oxford Review of Education,* 21 (4), 409–423.

Hedgecoe, A. (2016) "Reputational risk, academic freedom and research ethics review". *Sociology,* 50(3), 486–501.

Hedges, C. (2009) *Empire of Illusion.* New York. Nation Books.

Hieronymus, F. Lisinksi, A., Nilsson, S. and Eriksson, E. (2017) "Efficacy of selective serotonin reuptake inhibitors in the absence of side effects: a mega-analysis of citalopram and paroxetine in adult depression". *Molecular Psychiatry.* 25 July. DOI 10.1038/mp.2017.147. http://www.nature.com/mp/journal/vaop/ncurrent/full/mp2017147a.html?foxtrotcallback=true. Accessed September 2017.

Huxley, A. (1994) *Brave New World.* London. Vintage.

Illich, I. (2002) *Deschooling society.* London. Marion Boyars.

Independent (1998) "Honesty has not proved to be the best policy for whistle-blowers in higher education. But is all that set to change?" *The Independent,* 10 June. http://www.independent.co.uk/life-style/fear-is-the-key-to-naming-and-shaming-1164120.html Accessed July 2017.

Independent (2009a) "Scandal of the students who never sat exams". *The Independent*, 26 November. http://www.independent.co.uk/news/education/higher/scandal-of-the-students-who-never-sat-exams-1827307.html Accessed July 2017.

Independent (2009b) "Trouble at the top: Malcolm Gillies' departure from City University has revealed an intense relationship between governors and vice-chancellors". *The Independent*, 12 August. http://www.independent.co.uk/news/education/higher/trouble-at-the-top-malcolm-gillies-departure-from-city-university-has-revealed-an-intense-1771004.html Accessed July 2017.

Institute of Fiscal Studies (2017) "Higher education funding in England: past, present and options for the future". IFS Briefing Note BN211 https://www.ifs.org.uk/uploads/publications/bns/BN211.pdf Accessed July 2017.

Izak, M., Kostera, M. and Zawadzki, M. (2017) *The future of university education*. Houndmills. Palgrave MacMillan.

Jarvis, D. (2017) "Stressed teachers offered electric shock therapy to combat anxiety and depression". http://www.telegraph.co.uk/education/2017/07/01/stressed-teachers-offered-electric-shock-therapy-combat-anxiety Accessed July 2017.

Jenkin, T. (2017) 134. "The number of suicides at British universities before anyone started to notice". *The Tab*. https://thetab.com/uk/2017/04/13/number-suicides-took-people-listen-37297 Accessed April 2017.

Kurzweil, R. (2005) *The singularity is near*. New York. Viking.

Haywood, H. Jenkins, R. and Molesworth, M. (2011) "A degree will make all your dreams come true: higher education as the management of consumer desires". In M. Molesworth, R. Scullion and E. Nixon (eds) *The marketisation of teaching and learning in higher education* (pp.183–195). New York. Routledge.

Hesse, H. (2012) *Steppenwolf*. London. Penguin.

Kafka, F. (2014) *The Essential Kafka*. Ware. Wordsworth Editions.

Karran, T. and Mallinson, L. (2017) "Academic Freedom in the UK: Legal and Normative Protection in a Comparative Context". Report for the University and College Union. https://www.ucu.org.uk/media/8614/Academic-Freedom-in-the-UK-Legal-and-Normative-Protection-in-a-Comparative-Context-Report-for-UCU-Terence-Karran-and-Lucy-Mallinson-May-17/pdf/ucu_academicfreedomstudy_report_may17.pdf Accessed July 2017.

Kim, Y (2011) "Idol republic: the global emergence of girl industries and the commercialisation of girl bodies". *Journal of Gender Studies*, 20(4), 333–345.

Kirsch, I. (2009) *The Emperor's New Drugs. Exploding the Anti-Depressant Myth*. London. The Bodley Head.

Khomami, N. (2017) "Fourth MP quits Bath University role over vice-chancellor's pay". *The Guardian*, 22 August. https://www.theguardian.com/education/2017/aug/22/two-more-mps-quit-bath-university-roles-over-vice-chancellors-pay Accessed August 2017.

Klein, N. (2010) *No Logo*. London. Fourth Estate.

Krebs, C.P., Lindquist, C.H., Warner, T.D., Fisher, B.S. and Martin, S.L. (2007) "The Campus Sexual Assault (CSA) Study". National Institute of Justice. Washington. https://www.ncjrs.gov/pdffiles1/nij/grants/221153.pdf Accessed August 2017.

Krusi, A., Chettiar, J., Ridgway, A., Abbott, J., Strathdee, S.A., and Shannon, K. (2012) "Negotiating Safety and Sexual Risk Reduction with Clients in Unsanctioned Safer Indoor Sex Work Environments: A Qualitative Study", *Research and Practice*, 102(6), 1154–1159.

Kumar, A. (2011) "Achievements and limitations of the UK student movement". In M. Bailey and D. Freedman. *The assault on universities* (pp.132–142). London. Pluto Press.

Lantz, S. (2004). "Sex work and study: The new demands facing young people and their implications for health and well-being". *Traffic*, 3.

Lantz S. (2005) "Students Working in the Melbourne Sex Industry: Education, Human Capital and the Changing Patterns of the Youth Labour Market". *Journal of Youth Studies*, 8(4): 385–401.

Lees, P. (2014) "I couldn't have paid for uni without having sex for money". http://www.vice.com/en_uk/read/supporting-myself-through-university-by-having-sex-for-money?utm_source=vicefbuk. Accessed February 2014.

Lenton, P. (2015) "Determining student satisfaction: An economic analysis of the National Student Survey". *Economics of Education Review,* 47, 118–125.

Long, S.L., Mollen, D. and Smith, N.G. (2012) "College Women's Attitudes Toward Sex Workers". *Sex Roles,* 66, 117–127.

Mandela, N. (1994) *Long walk to freedom*. London. Little Brown and Company.

Marginson, S. (2006) "Dynamics of national and global competition in higher education", *Higher Education,* 52, 1–39.

McGettigan, A. (2013) *The great university gamble. Money markets and the future of higher education*. London. Pluto Press.

McLeod, E. (1982). *Working women: Prostitution now*. London. Croon Helm.

McNair, B. (2002) *Striptease culture: Sex, media and the democratization of desire*. London. Routledge.

McNeil, K. (2002) "The war on academic freedom" https://www.thenation.com/article/war-academic-freedom/ Accessed July 2017.

McQuillan, M. (2017) "Never mind the students, tuition fees are a bad deal for the taxpayer". https://www.theguardian.com/education/2017/oct/03/students-tuition-fees-taxpayer-government-borrow#comment-106189463 Accessed October 2017.

Milne, J. (2006) "Female students turn to prostitution to pay fees". *Sunday Times*, 8 October.

Moffat, P. G., and Peters, S. A. (2004). "Pricing personal services: An empirical study of earnings in the UK prostitution industry". *Scottish Journal of Political Economy*, 51, 675–690.

Monaghan, A. and Weale, S. (2017) "UK student loan debt soars to more than £100bn". https://www.theguardian.com/money/2017/jun/15/uk-student-loan-debt-soars-to-more-than-100bn Accessed July 2017.

Monbiot, G. (2017) "A despot in disguise: one man's mission to rip up democracy". *The Guardian*, 22 July https://www.theguardian.com/commentisfree/2017/jul/19/despot-disguise-democracy-james-mcgill-buchanan-totalitarian-capitalism Accessed July 2017.

Moncrieff, J. (2008) *The myth of the chemical cure*. Houndmills. Palgrave.

Morris, T., Dorling, D. and Davey Smith, G. (2016) "How well can we predict educational outcomes? Examining the roles of cognitive ability and social position in educational attainment". *Contemporary Social Science*, 11 (2–3), 154–168.

National Committee of Inquiry into Higher Education (1997) https://bei.leeds.ac.uk/Partners/NCIHE/ Accessed March 2009.

National Union of Students (2016) "Student Sex Worker Research". London.

Nietzsche, F. (1968) *Twilight of the idols*. London. Penguin.

Nursing Standard (1995) "Students resort to prostitution". *Nursing Standard*, 9 (39), 50. http://journals.rcni.com/doi/pdfplus/10.7748/ns.9.39.50.s49 Accessed July 2017.

Parini, J. (2017) "Noam Chomsky's 'Responsibility of Intellectuals' after 50 years: It's an even heavier responsibility now". *Salon*, 11 February. http://www.salon.com/2017/02/11/noam-chomskys-responsibility-of-intellectuals-after-50-years-its-an-even-heavier-responsibility-now/ Accessed Sep 2017.

Parker, I. (2014) "Austerity in the university". *The Psychologist*, 27(45), 236–238.

Parker, I. (2017) *Revolutionary keywords for a new left*. Winchester.

Zero Books.

Parr, C. (2014) "Nobel Laureates 'lost on Essex'". *Times Higher Education*, 2173, 9 October.

Pells, R. (2017a) "Student satisfaction levels fall amid nation-wide protests against rising tuition fees". *The Independent*, 10 August. http://www.independent.co.uk/student/news/students-boycott-national-student-survey-protest-against-higher-tuition-fees-decline-nus-tef-a7883221.html Accessed August 2017.

Pells, R. (2017b) "Sussex University failed duty of care to student assault victim, inquiry finds". *The Independent*, 18 January. http://www.independent.co.uk/news/uk/home-news/sussex-university-student-assault-allison-smith-senior-lecturer-dr-lee-salter-beat-punch-stamp-a7533751.html Accessed August 2017.

Penny, L. (2011) *Meat market. Female flesh under capitalism.* Winchester. Zero Books.

Pickard, J. (2005) Minutes of the meeting of the Faculty Research Ethics Sub-Committee, Wednesday 8 December 2004 at 2pm in EM336.

Piff, P.K., Stancato, D.M., Cote, S., Mendoza-Denton, R. and Keltner, D. (2012) "Higher social class predicts increased unethical behaviour". *Proceedings of the National Academy of Sciences USA 109*(11), 4086–4091.

Prestridge, J. (2013) "My £39,000 debt will never get repaid: Debt time-bomb for taxpayers as 85% of students will never pay off loans". http://www.thisismoney.co.uk/money/cardsloans/article-2326560/Debt-timebomb-85-cent-students-pay-loans.html. Accessed May 2013.

Rabinow, P. (1991) *The Foucault Reader*. London. Penguin.

Rees, L. (2005) *The Nazis. A warning from history*. London. BBC Books.

Rhodes, A. (2016) "Our education system is prejudiced against white, working class boys – it's time to empower them". *The

Guardian, 9 June. http://www.independent.co.uk/voices/our-education-system-is-inherently-prejudiced-against-white-working-class-boys-its-time-to-empower-a7072821.html Accessed September 2017.

Rhodes, C. (2015) "Academic freedom in the corporate university: Squandering our inheritance". In M. Izak, M. Kostera and Zawadski, M. (eds) (2017) *The future of university education* (pp.19–38). Houndmills. Palgrave.

Richardson. T, Elliot, P., Roberts, R. and Jansen, M. (2017) "A Longitudinal Study of Financial Difficulties and Mental Health in a National Sample of British Undergraduate Students". *Community Mental Health Journal*, 53(3), 344–352.

Roberts, R. (1999) "Debts of Despair". *The Guardian, Higher Education*, vi–vii.

Roberts, R. (2010) "Researching Students in Sex Work: Market Values and Academic Freedom". *Journal of Critical Psychology, Counselling and Psychotherapy*, 10(1), 12–17.

Roberts, R. (2015) *Psychology and Capitalism*. Winchester. Zero Books.

Roberts, R. (2017) *The Off-Modern: Psychology Estranged*. Winchester. Zero Books.

Roberts, R., Golding, J., Towell, T. and Weinreb, I. (1999) "The Effects of Students' Economic Circumstances on British Students' Mental and Physical Health". *Journal of American College Health*, 48, 103–109.

Roberts, R., Golding, J., Towell, T. Reid, S., Woodford, S., Vetere, A. and Weinreb, I. (2000) "Mental and physical health in students: The role of economic circumstances". *British Journal of Health Psychology*, 5(3), 289–297.

Roberts, R., Bergstrom, S. and La Rooy, D. (2007a) "Commentary: UK Students and Sex Work: Current Knowledge and Research Issues". *Journal of Community and Applied Social Psychology*, 17, 141–146.

Roberts, R., Bergstrom, S. and La Rooy, D. (2007b) "Sex Work and Students: An Exploratory Study". *Journal of Further and Higher Education*, 31(4), 323–334.

Roberts, R., Jones, A. and Sanders, T. (2013) "The relationship between sex work and students in the UK: Providers and Purchasers". *Sex Education: Sexuality, Society and Learning*, 13(3) 349–363.

Ryan, J. and Sackrey, C. (1984) *Strangers in paradise. Academics from the working class*. Boston. South End Press.

Sagar, T., and Jones, D. (2012). "Interactive health: Student sex workers' project (Big Lottery)". Swansea University's Centre for Criminal Justice and Criminology. http://www.swansea. ac.uk/law/criminology/researchcentre/ Accessed November 20, 2012.

Sagar, T, Jones, E, Jones, D. and Clark, L. (2014) "Sex Work Research Wales 2010–2014". Swansea University.

Sagar, T., Jones, D., Symons, K., Bowring, J. and Roberts, R. (2015) "Student participation in the sex industry: higher education response and staff experiences and perceptions". *Journal of Higher Education Policy and Management*, 37(4), 400–412.

Sagar, T., Jones, D., Symons, K., Bowring, J. and Roberts, R. (2016) "Student involvement in the sex industry: Findings from the United Kingdom identifying motivations and experiences". *British Journal of Sociology. DOI: 10.1111/1468-4446.12216.*

Said, E. (1996) *Representations of the intellectual*. New York. Vintage Books.

Sanders, T. (2004) "A Continuum of Risk? The Management of Health, Physical and Emotional Risks by Female Sex Workers". *Sociology of Health and Illness*, 26(5), 557–574.

Sanders, T. (2007) "Becoming an ex-sex worker: Making transitions out of a deviant career". *Feminist Criminology*, 2 (1), 74–95.

Sanders, T. (2008) *Paying for pleasure. Men who buy sex*. Cullompton. Willan Publishing.

Sanders, T. and 26 others (2008) "An academic response to Big

Brothel". Available at http://www.uknswp.org/wp-content/uploads/AcademicResponseBigBrothelFinSept2008.pdf

Sanders, T. (2012) "The advantages and attractions of informality: Sex industry work among migrants and students in the UK". In P. Ponsaers, P. Saitta, and J. Shapland (eds) *Formal, informal, and criminal economy: An outlook on Northern and Southern Europe* Leeds. Eleven Press.

Sanders, T. and Campbell, R. (2012) "Sex entertainment venues regulating working conditions: Impact Report". University of Leeds School of Sociology and Social Policy. ESRC Report.

Sanders, T. and Campbell, R. (2014) "Criminalization, protection and rights: Global tensions in the governance of commercial sex". *Criminology and Criminal Justice*, 14(5), 535–548.

Sanders, T. and Hardy, K. (2012) "Devalued, deskilled and diversified: Explaining the proliferation of lap dancing in the UK". *British Journal of Sociology* 63 (3), 513–532.

Sanders, T. and Hardy, K. (2015) "Students selling sex: marketisation, higher education and consumption". *British Journal of Sociology, 36(5), 747–765.

Sanders, T., Cunningham, S., Platt, L., Grenfell, P. and Macioti, P.G. (2017) "Reviewing the occupational risks of sex workers in comparison to other 'risky' professions". Welcome Trust. University of Leicester. London School of Hygiene and Tropical Medicine.

Scambler, G. (2007) "Sex work stigma: opportunist migrants in London". *Sociology*, 41(6), 1079–1096.

Schekman, R. (2013) "How journals like Nature, Cell and Science are damaging science". *The Independent*, 9 December. http://www.theguardian.com/commentisfree/2013/dec/09/how-journals-nature-science-cell-damage-science Accessed December 2013.

Scott, P. (2010) "Tuition fees rises: are university vice-chancellors to blame?" *The Guardian,* 22 November. https://www.theguardian.com/education/2010/nov/22/tuition-fees-higher-education Accessed November 2010.

Scott, P. (2017) "The end of tuition fees is on the horizon - universities must get ready". *The Guardian*, 4 July. https://www.theguardian.com/education/2017/jul/04/end-tuition-fees-universities-get-ready#comment-101499506. Accessed July 2017.

Scoular, J. (2004) "The 'Subject' of Prostitution: Interpreting the Discursive, Symbolic and Material Position of Sex/work in Feminist Theory". *Feminist Theory* 5(3), 343–355.

Sedgman, J. (2004) "Sex work more attractive option for students". *The World Today*, ABC. April.

Senett, R. and Cobb, J. (1973) *The hidden injuries of class*. New York. Vintage Books.

Streeck, W. (2016) *How will capitalism end?* London. Verso.

Shepherd, J. (2011) "Student debt nears £60,000 for 2012 university freshers, survey predicts". http://www.theguardian.com/money/2011/aug/12/student-debt-to-rocket-2012-freshers Accessed August 2011.

Szasz, T. (1960) "The myth of mental illness". *American Psychologist, 15*, 13–118.

Szasz, T. (1961) *The myth of mental illness*. New York. Harper and Row.

Szasz, T. (2001) *Pharmacracy: Medicine and politics in America.* London. Praeger.

Szasz, T. (2002) *Liberation by oppression: A comparative study of slavery and psychiatry.* New Brunswick, NJ. Transaction.

Tetlow, G. (2016) *Financial Times* (2016) "Two-thirds of UK students 'will never pay off debt'". *Financial Times*, 4 July.

The Telegraph (2008) "Kingston University students 'told to lie' to boost rankings". 14 May. http://www.telegraph.co.uk/news/1954847/Kingston-University-students-told-to-lie-to-boost-rankings.html Accessed July 2017.

The Telegraph (2012) "London Met banned from issuing visas to foreign students". http://www.telegraph.co.uk/news/

uknews/immigration/9508115/London-Met-banned-from-issuing-visas-to-foreign-students.html. Accessed July 2017.

Thorley, C. (2017) "Improving Student Mental Health in the UK's universities". IPPR. London. https://www.ippr.org/files/2017-09/1504645674_not-by-degrees-170905.pdf Accessed September 2017.

Times Higher Education (2001) "Students in Leeds tarred by sex myth". Retrieved 27 March, 2009, http://www.timeshighereducation.co.uk/story.asp?sto ryCode=159597&sectioncode=26 Accessed March 2009.

Times Higher Education (2011) "Dean criticised by tribunal is promoted". *THE*, 28 July. https://www.timeshighereducation.com/news/dean-criticised-by-tribunal-is-promoted/416955.article?sectioncode=26&storycode=416955&c=1 Accessed July 2015.

Times Higher Education (2012) "London Met UCU returns 'no confidence' vote on v-c". *THE*, 24 April. https://www.timeshighereducation.com/news/london-met-ucu-returns-no-confidence-vote-on-v-c/419741.article?storycode=419741 Accessed July 2017.

Times Higher Education (2015) "Academics in the minority at more than two-thirds of UK universities". *THE*, 3 September. https://www.timeshighereducation.com/news/academics-minority-more-two-thirds-uk-universities Accessed August 2017.

Tucker, (2012) Bully U. "Central planning and higher education". *The Independent Review*, 17 (1), 99-119.

Turner, C. (2017) "Investigation into University of Sussex lecturer unearths further reports of alleged harassment and sexual abuse". *The Telegraph*, 18 January http://www.telegraph.co.uk/education/2017/01/18/investigation-university-sussexlecturer-finds-history-harassment/ Accessed August 2017.

UCA News (1990) "Students turn to 'prostitution' to pay university fees". http://www.ucanews.com/story-archive/?post_name=/ 1999/12/09/students-turn-to-prostituition-to-pay-university-fees&post_id=14965 Accessed July 2017.

UCU (2008) RAE 2008. http://www.ucu.org.uk/index.cfm? articleid=1442 (Accessed March 7, 2009).

UCU (2015) "The prevent duty. A guide for branches and members". https://www.ucu.org.uk/media/7370/The-prevent-du-ty-guidance-for-branches-Dec-15/pdf/ucu_preventdutyguid-ance_dec15.pdf Accessed July 2017.

UCU (2017) "Academic Freedom in 2017". https://www.ucu.org. uk/academic-freedom-in-2017 Accessed July 2017.

UNESCO (1997) "Recommendation concerning the Status of Higher-Education Teaching Personnel". 11 November. http:// portal.unesco.org/en/ev.php-URL_ID=13144&URL_DO=DO_ TOPIC&URL_SECTION=201.html Accessed July 2017.

Universities UK. (2016) "Higher education in facts and figures 2016". London. http://www.universitiesuk.ac.uk/facts-and-stats/data-and-analysis/Documents/facts-and-figures-2016. pdf Accessed July 2017

Wallis, L. (2013) "Is 25 the new cut-off point for adulthood?" http:// www.bbc.co.uk/newsmagazine-24173194 Accessed September 2013.

Weale, S. (2017) "Advertising watchdog forces Reading University to ditch 'top 1%' claim". *The Guardian*, 8 June. https://www.theguardian.com/education/2017/jun/08/ advertising-watchdog-forces-reading-university-to-ditch-top-1-claim Accessed June 2017.

Weitzer, R. (Ed.) (2000) *Sex For Sale: Prostitution, Pornography and the Sex Industry.* London: Routledge.

Wexo (2013) "Graduate debt research". http://www.wexo.co.uk/ blog/?p=2878 Accessed August 2013.

Williams, J. (2015) "The National Student Survey should be abolished before it dos any more harm". *The Guardian*, 13 August. https://www.theguardian.com/higher-education-network/2015/aug/13/the-national-student-survey-should-be-abolished-before-it-does-any-more-harm Accessed August 2017.

Winters, J.A. (2011) *Oligarchy*. New York. Cambridge University Press.

Wolkowitz, C., Cohen, R. L., Sanders, T. and Hardy, K. (2013) *Body/Sex/Work. Intimate, embodied and sexualized labour*. Houndmills. Palgrave Macmillan.

Zamora, D. and Behrent, M.C. (eds) (2016) *Foucault and Neoliberalism*. London. Polity.

Also by the author

The Off-Modern: Psychology Estranged
Zero Books, 2017
ISBN: 978-1-78535-595-0
Society is undergoing a process of deep change and
transformation as the neoliberal order moves into crisis.
Contemporary psychology, mired in exceptionalism and
individualism, fails to address this broader context and
continues with a fragmented reductionist approach. *The Off-
Modern* draws on the work of Svetlana Boym to suggest a
new way of 'doing' psychology which challenges not only
the existing epistemological and reductionist outlook but the
centrality of a scientific professional discourse as a suitable
vehicle for improving lives and making sense of the world.

Psychology and Capitalism: The Manipulation of Mind
Zero Books, 2015
ISBN: 978-1-78279-654-1
Psychology and Capitalism is a critical and accessible account
of the ideological and material role of psychology in
supporting capitalist enterprise and, through the promotion
of individualism, holding individuals entirely responsible for
their fate.

Zero Books

CULTURE, SOCIETY & POLITICS

Contemporary culture has eliminated the concept and public figure of the intellectual. A cretinous anti-intellectualism presides, cheer-led by hacks in the pay of multinational corporations who reassure their bored readers that there is no need to rouse themselves from their stupor. Zer0 Books knows that another kind of discourse – intellectual without being academic, popular without being populist – is not only possible: it is already flourishing. Zer0 is convinced that in the unthinking, blandly consensual culture in which we live, critical and engaged theoretical reflection is more important than ever before.

If you have enjoyed this book, why not tell other readers by posting a review on your preferred book site.

Recent bestsellers from Zero Books are:

In the Dust of This Planet
Horror of Philosophy vol. 1
Eugene Thacker
In the first of a series of three books on the Horror of
Philosophy, *In the Dust of This Planet* offers the genre of horror
as a way of thinking about the unthinkable.
Paperback: 978-1-84694-676-9 ebook: 978-1-78099-010-1

Capitalist Realism
Is there no alternative?
Mark Fisher
An analysis of the ways in which capitalism has presented itself
as the only realistic political-economic system.
Paperback: 978-1-84694-317-1 ebook: 978-1-78099-734-6

Rebel Rebel
Chris O'Leary
David Bowie: every single song. Everything you want to know,
everything you didn't know.
Paperback: 978-1-78099-244-0 ebook: 978-1-78099-713-1

Cartographies of the Absolute
Alberto Toscano, Jeff Kinkle
An aesthetics of the economy for the twenty-first century.
Paperback: 978-1-78099-275-4 ebook: 978-1-78279-973-3

Malign Velocities
Accelerationism and Capitalism
Benjamin Noys
Long listed for the Bread and Roses Prize 2015, *Malign Velocities* argues against the need for speed, tracking acceleration as the symptom of the ongoing crises of capitalism.
Paperback: 978-1-78279-300-7 ebook: 978-1-78279-299-4

Meat Market
Female Flesh under Capitalism
Laurie Penny
A feminist dissection of women's bodies as the fleshy fulcrum of capitalist cannibalism, whereby women are both consumers and consumed.
Paperback: 978-1-84694-521-2 ebook: 978-1-84694-782-7

Poor but Sexy
Culture Clashes in Europe East and West
Agata Pyzik
How the East stayed East and the West stayed West.
Paperback: 978-1-78099-394-2 ebook: 978-1-78099-395-9

Romeo and Juliet in Palestine
Teaching Under Occupation
Tom Sperlinger
Life in the West Bank, the nature of pedagogy and the role of a university under occupation.
Paperback: 978-1-78279-637-4 ebook: 978-1-78279-636-7

Sweetening the Pill
or How we Got Hooked on Hormonal Birth Control
Holly Grigg-Spall
Has contraception liberated or oppressed women? *Sweetening the Pill* breaks the silence on the dark side of hormonal contraception.
Paperback: 978-1-78099-607-3 ebook: 978-1-78099-608-0

Why Are We The Good Guys?
Reclaiming your Mind from the Delusions of Propaganda
David Cromwell
A provocative challenge to the standard ideology that Western power is a benevolent force in the world.
Paperback: 978-1-78099-365-2 ebook: 978-1-78099-366-9

Readers of ebooks can buy or view any of these bestsellers by clicking on the live link in the title. Most titles are published in paperback and as an ebook. Paperbacks are available in traditional bookshops. Both print and ebook formats are available online.

Find more titles and sign up to our readers' newsletter at http://www.johnhuntpublishing.com/culture-and-politics

Follow us on Facebook at https://www.facebook.com/ZeroBooks

and Twitter at https://twitter.com/Zer0Books